THE EFFECTIVE HEALTH CARE EXECUTIVE

A Guide to a Winning Management Style

Contributors

Robert C. Bills

Donald S. Buckley

Newell E. France

David A. Gee

Pat N. Groner

Kevin G. Halpern

Sheldon S. King

William C. Mason

Boone Powell, Jr.

J. Larry Read

Austin Ross

Arlene A. Sargent

Ken W. Sargent

Bruce E. Spivey, M.D.

Carol D. Teig

Lois M. Tow

Robert L. Wall

Dan S. Wilford

THE EFFECTIVE HEALTH CARE EXECUTIVE

A Guide to a Winning Management Style

Edited by

Terence F. Moore
President
Mid-Michigan Health Care Systems
Midland, Michigan

Earl A. Simendinger, PhD
President and CEO
St. Luke's Hospital
San Francisco, California

AN ASPEN PUBLICATION®
Aspen Publishers, Inc.   1986   Rockville, Maryland
Royal Tunbridge Wells

362.1
E 271

Library of Congress Cataloging in Publication Data

The Effective health care executive.

"An Aspen publication."
Includes bibliographies and index.
1. Hospitals—Administration   2. Health services administration.
I. Moore, Terence F.   II. Simendinger, Earl A.
RA971.E34   1986   362.1'068   86-13973
ISBN: 0-87189-386-X

Editorial Services: Marsha Davies

Library of Congress Catalog Card Number: 86-13973
ISBN: 0-87189-386-X

Printed in the United States of America

1 2 3 4 5

To

Earl A. Simendinger, M.D., and Leah Simendinger
Albert A. Moore, Marilla H. Moore,
and Carleen K. Moore

Table of Contents

Preface

The attention being paid to managerial effectiveness and success in the management literature, especially at the chief executive officer level, has never been greater. Some of the more important books published recently on managerial effectiveness and leadership are: *Peak Performance: The New Heroes of American Business,* by Charles Garfield, and *Leaders: The Strategies for Taking Charge,* by Warren Bennis. The 1986 American College of Health Care Executives' book award went to *CEO: Corporate Leadership in Action,* by Henry Levinson. Although all of these are useful, none are oriented specifically to health care executives. They do not address many of the issues that are unique to health care administration such as administrative/medical relationships and the CEOs' role in the community.

When we began to analyze the traits and style that make health care executives successful, we considered doing an extensive questionnaire and combining the results with a literature review, but this has been done already and our comments would have added little to existing knowledge. We also considered the possibility of joining with a group of academicians to develop a book about the traits that make for effective executives. Fortunately, we discussed this issue first with many of our colleagues. It became clear that the individuals best able to address the many elements of style that contribute to the success or failure of health care executives are the executives who themselves have reached the top of their professions.

Many of us have been fortunate enough to work with and learn from such highly effective health care executive individuals as Ted Bowen and James Harding, but there are many others in the field who can help practitioners and students at all levels, not only by their example but by documenting their perceptions of various aspects of administrative style.

Consequently, we asked a number of well-known hospital chief executive officers in the United States to document their thoughts on some aspect of

administrative style. All of these executives have been exceptionally successful in their respective institutions. Moreover, all have held significant
leadership positions in the health care field, generally, in addition to their
roles in their institutions. They represent a geographic cross-section of the
United States and a diversity of management style.

This book is not a prescription for success. It is, rather, a series of
observations and studies of the factors that are recognized as contributing to
or detracting from an effective management style.

We encourage readers to reflect on the examples of health care executives
they know who have been successful, as well as on the techniques they
themselves have used effectively. It is our sincere hope that the wisdom and
observations of these authors will be of value to those who must perform in
an increasingly competitive environment.

Terence F. Moore
Earl A. Simendinger

Acknowledgments

We wish to extend our deep appreciation to the authors of the various chapters who made this book possible. Each made a significant commitment in time and effort to make the necessary deadlines and develop their respective chapters in spite of their hectic schedules. Peggy Carter provided invaluable assistance in the coordination of the project. The staff of Aspen Publishers, particularly Barbara Tansill, Editor, Sandy Cannon, Assistant Editor, Marsha Davies, Editorial Assistant, and all those who reviewed and revised the numerous drafts of the manuscript, deserve special credit. We are grateful for their efforts and support.

Charisma: What It Is and How To Get It

Kevin G. Halpern

1

Charisma: Some have it and some don't. John F. Kennedy, Ronald Reagan, Franklin D. Roosevelt, and Lee Iacocca all are leaders who possessed and/or possess charisma. However, charisma is not a prerequisite for successful leadership. It could be argued that Richard Nixon, Lyndon Johnson, and Henry Ford II did not have charisma, yet they were very effective business and political leaders. Leaders always are looking for that competitive edge in business. Charismatic chief executive officers have one important advantage. The people around them work harder and longer because they believe in the value system and mission articulated by their CEOs. Employees perform better and are willing to sacrifice more because they have bought into the dream of the man at the top.

Charisma is defined in one of the numerous Webster's dictionaries as "a personal magic of leadership arousing special popular loyalty or enthusiasm for a public figure" or as "a special magnetic charm or appeal." When people think of a charismatic individual, they think in terms of that person's magnetism, allure, presence, charm, attraction, and zeal. To understand charisma and the charismatic leader, it is necessary first to explore what it is that makes a leader charismatic and, second, find ways to internalize those skills and/or characteristics into personal management styles.

Research into the charismatic phenomenon has taken place primarily in the fields of sociology, psychology, and political science. Sociology offers the preeminent body of information on the subject, distantly followed by psychohistorical text and articles. The nature of the disciplines analyzing charisma would suggest that this phenomenon is a result of:

- a form of legitimate authority being vested in the charismatic individual

- the extreme excitement generated by the charismatic individual or object and its effects on the person(s) coming into contact with this excited state
- the manifest perception of the charismatic performer by the members who form that individual's community.

CHARISMA: WHAT IS IT?

Religious Foundations

It is not possible to explore the literature on charisma without encountering the definitions and structural framework proposed by Max Weber. He originally defined charisma from his observations of charismatic movements in religion. He postulated there were three types of charisma in this sphere: magical, prophetic, and routinized.

Weber defined magical charisma as the ability to accomplish the extraordinary through means that are perceived as not available to the general populace. The faith healer's ability to cure the lame in and of itself would be an example of magical charisma. It was this "grace," divine intervention, or ability to accomplish the inexplicable that caused extreme excitement for both the performer and the audience.

Prophetic charisma involves not only extraordinariness but also an element of idea and doctrine. Weber qualifies the nature of the idea by saying that "a prophetic revelation involves a unified view of the world derived from a consciously integrated meaningful attitude toward life."[1] In religion, it is the personal call of the charismatic leader who through divine revelation, vision, or compelling mission calls the audience to serve. Leaders of the prophetic genre rarely are officeholders but come to power by filling a void caused by the lack of charisma in the authority structure. Martin Luther King, Jr. and Mohandas K. Gandhi are two examples of this form of charismatic leadership. Although neither held office in the formal power structure, their ability to mobilize the masses was demonstrated time and time again.

The charismatic leader challenges the normative order. This individual's message sets aside the old order and beckons others to "follow me." To transform those followers, the charismatic leader, either through exemplary behavior or the excitement caused by the message, must create a stark contrast between the accepted values of society and the new order.

The all-encompassing power of the charismatic leader stems from the followers' duty to obey rather than to have a choice as to accepting that individual's authority. Weber expressed it as follows:

The holder of charisma seizes the task that is adequate for him and demands obedience and a following by virtue of his mission. . . . If those to whom he feels he has been sent recognize him, he is their master—so long as he knows how to maintain recognition through proving himself. But he does not derive his "right" from their will, in the manner of an election. Rather, the reverse holds: It is the duty of those to whom he addresses his mission to recognize him as their charismatically qualified leader.[2]

Weber distinguished magical charisma and prophetic charisma as being forms of "real" charisma—products of singularly unique individuals who, through their ability to create an extreme excitement in themselves and those around them, are able to convert others into a charismatic community. It is the ability to create extreme excitement in themselves and their audiences that makes the magicians or prophets charismatic. The magic, mission, or revelation may be the cause of the excitement but it is the excited state that galvanizes the audience to the charismatic leader.

Routinized charisma is charisma transformed. It is charisma institutionalized, organized, and somehow passed down and therefore does not contain the revolutionary attributes found in the other types. Routinized charisma by its very nature does not include the gift of grace or intensely excited state of either magical or prophetic charisma. It lacks the uniqueness of belonging to a particular individual; rather, it usually is infused in an office or position. Priests represent a form of routinized charisma in that the charisma of their office contains an aspect of mission that is present in prophetic charisma. Simply stated, routinization is the process by which charisma becomes integrated into the normative order.

Form of Legitimate Domination

Classical management theory holds that power is the ability of an individual or group to get some other individual or group to change in some manner.[3] Authority is the right to act.[4] That is to say, it is legitimate power vested in a particular person or position and accepted as appropriate and recognized as legitimate not only by the power wielder but also by those over whom it is wielded.[5] As a part of his classical definition of legitimate domination, Weber developed three devices by which power was legitimated, terming them traditional authority, legal-rational authority, and charismatic authority.

The concept of traditional authority is based upon power that is accepted because it is inherent, longstanding, and preordained. The Pope and hereditary kings are examples of personages who derive their authority through traditional domination. In the Roman Catholic Church, the power of the Pope over the Church has been established over the past two millenniums and his right to exercise it is now considered intrinsic to the position he holds as the anointed of God here on Earth.

The power of hereditary kings or queens is likewise accepted by those over whom they rule by virtue of their peoples' acceptance of a tradition in which authority is transformed through lineage. In both cases, obedience is owed to the person holding the traditionally legitimized position, who in turn is bound by tradition and precedent.

Legal-rational authority is based upon power that is accepted because of the rules and regulations established within the social order. In the case of legal-rational authority, power resides in the office and not the officeholder. The extent of the officeholder's power to act is limited to the area ascribed to the office by the rules and regulations that established the position.

Charismatic authority is power that is accepted because of the personal qualities of the individual. Weber's discussions on legitimate authority gave rise to two similar yet distinct definitions of charismatic leadership. He defined charisma as:

1. . . . a certain quality of an individual personality by virtue of which he is considered extraordinary and treated as endowed with supernatural, superhuman, or at least specifically exceptional powers and qualities. These are such as are not accessible to the ordinary person, but are regarded as of divine origin or as exemplary, and on the basis of them is treated as a leader.
   . . . What is alone important is how the individual is actually regarded by those subject to charismatic authority, by his followers or disciples.[6]

2. . . . a personal quality which turned whoever possessed it into an impressive personality. This quality was inborn and extraordinary and was, in a twofold sense, not a part of the normative order or everyday activity: it had no pattern; it was exceptional in the sense that not everyone could achieve it since it could not be learned; and it had no symbolization preceding its actual occurrence and was thus frequently symbolized retrospectively as extraordinary, meaning superhuman.[7]

Genuine charismatic authority, as thus defined, had five key ingredients:

1. Charisma is an individual ability that could not be learned or taught. However, it could lie dormant and be awakened or suddenly recognized because of changes in the social structure.

2. A leader/follower relationship dictates that members of the group, even those who may not have had direct contact with the leader, feel closely aligned with both the leader and the cause.
3. The leader must be perceived as extraordinary or exceptional by those who surround the person.
4. The charismatic authority figure must maintain a sense of mission, guiding purpose, or absolute values that serve as a binding force within the charismatic community.
5. Pure charisma, as well as the individual personifying it, must by definition be revolutionary. It must differentiate itself from the normative values of the existing social structure as well as everyday social institutions.

Charisma is sought after in the fields of religion, politics, and management because it gives the individual possessing it the unquestioned right to lead. Therefore, the right to exercise authority and discretion over the group by the charismatic leader is accepted willingly by its members because they perceive the individual as extraordinary, heroic, exemplary, or a savior. A leader who is considered charismatic usually is loved and revered by the followers and does not find it necessary to use force or other punitive means to achieve desired ends. Other agents such as fear, reward, and punishment are not necessary to induce the followers to obey the charismatic leader's commands. It is much easier to rule, govern, or manage when the audience is predisposed to accept the will of a leader. It is even better when the audience internalizes it as the will of an irresistible superhuman force.

Key to Weber's discussion of legitimacy and charismatic authority is the concept that the leaders must continue to prove themselves in the arena that they have proclaimed as their own. As long as they continue to prove themselves in this sphere and as long as their followers benefit from their leadership, then their right to exercise dominion over their followers remains intact. That is to say, "if proof of his charismatic qualification fails him for long, the leader endowed with charisma tends to think his god or his magical or heroic powers have deserted him. If he is for long unsuccessful, above all if his leadership fails to benefit his followers, it is likely that his charismatic authority will disappear."[8] Therefore, it can be inferred that charismatic authority is, at least partially, based on the followers receiving some benefit from the relationship. At this point the significance lies not in whether the benefit is conveyed tangibly, psychologically, socially, or otherwise, but in the fact that the followers perceive their relationship with the leader as beneficial. Should that beneficial relationship cease to exist for an extended time, the followers will become disheartened and the charismatic authority structure will be shaken.

The Routinization of Charisma

The routinization of charisma involves the process of transferring the authority of the genuine charismatic to another individual or group of individuals. The original leader derived power and authority by virtue of that person's mission, vision, or exemplary qualities; the transformation process involves imputing the perceived qualities of the legitimate leader to an individual, office, institution, or social or political structure. Sharot wrote: "The distinctive elements of 'pure' charisma, the concentration of a unique gift of grace in a single individual and the absence of routine procedures, will necessarily disappear, but the gift of grace may be transformed into a quality that is nevertheless acquirable, attached to an office, or to an institutional structure."[9] The process of transferring charisma may occur during the life of the leader or upon that person's death. Two well-known forms of routinized charisma are hereditary charisma and office charisma.

Hereditary charisma is based on the belief that charisma is a quality that could be transmitted by blood. That is to say, the bearer of charisma was perceived by followers as receiving the gift of grace genetically; therefore, it is conceivable that that gift could be shared with or transmitted to any heirs. For one who is the beneficiary of hereditary charisma, "recognition is no longer paid to the charismatic qualities of the individual, but to the legitimacy of the position he has acquired by hereditary succession. . . . This may lead in the direction either of traditionalization or of legalization . . . [where] hereditary monarchy is a conspicuous illustration."[10]

Office charisma is based on the premise that charisma can be transferred from one individual to another through ritual. In the case of office charisma, "the belief in legitimacy is no longer directed to the individual, but to the acquired qualities and to the effectiveness of the ritual acts. The most important example is the transmission of priestly charisma by anointing, consecration, or the laying on of hands: and of royal authority, by anointing and by coronation."[11]

The Transformation of Charismatic Leadership

For individuals to look at charisma in a way that allows them to acquire it, it is necessary to change the notion of charisma from the pure or genuine types that Weber defined to a more general approach based on the characteristics of charismatic leadership. The transformation process gives rise to a slightly different perception of charismatic leadership and it is this process that is utilized for the new definition here.

Charismatic leadership stems from a special gift that certain individuals possess. A charismatic leader is one who under difficult circumstances arouses individuals to greater heights than previously thought possible. This type of leadership inspires followers to put aside their fears and lethargy. When followers are feeling frightened, depressed, or beaten, this leader gives them the strength and courage to carry on. Charisma brings cohesion to the group when its confidence is shaken or when it is beset by inner turmoil. It is leadership that inspires confidence in the face of great odds and helps the charismatic community face the unknown, armed with the optimism and courage of the charismatic leader. Simplistically, it is leadership based upon the leader's ability to boost the group's morale as well as to maintain its cohesion.

Many devices have been used to symbolize the transformation process. In primitive cultures in which charisma tended to be magical, the witch doctor or charismatic high priest would teach an apprentice some of the leader's magic tricks that when performed would awe and inspire the villagers. Sometimes the primitive charismatic used large masks painted in ornate colors to give the illusion of otherworldliness. If a larger-than-life appearance was required, stilts were employed to give the effect of great stature. Some form of dance or ritual may have been performed to stimulate the audience visually and possibly cause a mesmerizing effect. Chants frequently were used to bombard the audio senses, with the beat and timbre manipulated to bring about an excited state among the members of the charismatic community. Any one or combination of the above were used to gain and maintain the authority of the primitive charismatic leader. In that none of these devices were genuinely charismatic but merely represented what the audience perceived as charismatic, they were transferable.

The charismatic tribal leader could pass the tricks, the costume, the chant, and the dance on to an heir. To the charismatic community at large, what was passed on was the ritual that routinized charisma and invested it not in the specific leader but in the bearer of the symbols perceived as charismatic. That is to say, over time the charismatic leader through the use of symbolism could cause the charismatic community to rely on the symbol(s) of charisma in place of the actual charisma the individual possessed. Often it is not the charismatic leader who personally transfers charisma to a successor but the disciples or hierarchy, who surrounded the leader and who wish to preserve their status, that develop the transformational mechanisms.

Even in more advanced cultures, symbolism is an important part of the transformation process. The pomp and circumstance of a coronation symbolizes the awe-inspiring transference of authority to a new king or queen. Usually the first king was a heroic warrior who inspired his men in battle through both deed and extraordinary military skills. The coronation ritual would be established to confer upon the heir the crown, the scepter, royal robe, and other artifacts that represented the authority of the charismatic king. The church usually played a strong role in the coronation, providing a ritual in which the heir was anointed to symbolize his being chosen by God, something not available to everyone and therefore considered extraordinary. After a number of successions, the authority of the latter-day kings may become derived more from traditional than from charismatic authority, but it still contains an element of charisma. Weber wrote:

> As domination congeals into a permanent structure, charisma recedes as a creative force. . . . However, charisma remains a very important element of the social structure, even though it is much transformed. . . . after its routinization, its very quality as an extraordinary, supernatural, and divine force makes it a suitable source of legitimate authority for the successors of the charismatic hero.[12]

CHARISMA: HOW TO GET IT

Charisma could not be learned or acquired, but merely awakened or recognized, under Weber's sociologic definition. This definition poses a problem in that it offers no way to acquire charisma. However, a more rational approach to looking at both the charismatic personality and authority structure may help resolve this dilemma.

First, it could be postulated that all individuals have within them an element of charisma awaiting a propitious time when the proper sociopsychological conditions are present to come to the forefront. For instance, the leader of a lynch mob can evoke passion and excitement in a crowd through his persuasive speech and extreme personal excitement, thus exercising charismatic authority within the context of the mob. However, he may never have shown leadership or charismatic tendencies before.

Second, the transformation process could be examined to determine the elements that make it possible for genuine charisma to be infused into routine social structures. Symbolism is a large part of the transformation process. The use of appropriate symbols, along with the practice and refinement of certain skills, could create the illusion of the persuasive personality found in the charismatic leader.

Third, a definition of charisma could be constructed, based on the attributes found common in charismatic personalities. Specifically, the traits must be identified. It then would be appropriate to discuss how those characteristics can be effectively obtained or represented to the manager's various constituencies.

THE ATTRIBUTES OF CHARISMA

Perhaps it could be best said that the attributes of charisma are in the eyes of the beholder. Certainly the moral standards of certain charismatic leaders like the late Jim Jones, the cult leader in Guyana, could be questioned by many; yet there was a man who dominated the lives of thousands through the use of his charisma.

Therefore, the characteristics of charisma must be viewed in a value-neutral sense. In that sense, charisma and charismatic authority have several major attributes that from a phenomenological perspective may shed some light on the subject. It should be noted that these characteristics run throughout Weber's works, especially those pertaining to genuine or pure charisma.

Power

Charismatic leaders undeniably are wielders of great power. As discussed, their authority is without bounds so long as they remain charismatically qualified. The attributes that afford them such authority are the abilities to (1) attract or fascinate others, (2) arouse a sympathetic response in others, and (3) motivate themselves as well as others to greater heights. From a sociopsychological perspective, Glassman refers to the "phenomenon of the 'blick,' the mutual look [that] can produce intense feelings and generate near-hypnotic states of consciousness in individuals and whole groups"[13] as one of the more powerful characteristics of charismatic leaders. Basically, the power of charisma lies in the leaders' ability to maintain their appeal and allure within their charismatic community.

CEOs customarily run their institutions using legal–rational authority. However, such power accrues to the office, not necessarily to the officeholder. If the executive is able to transcend the office and symbolically establish a presence throughout the institution, then the authority will be perceived as being derived from the officeholder individually. This perception will ensure the willing cooperation and participation of employees because it is their duty to follow the charismatic leader.

Presence

The charismatic leaders' presence will be established throughout the charismatic organization. Individually, they bring with them a quality of poise and effectiveness that will enable them to achieve a close relationship with their audience. The leader/follower relationship is one of attraction and intimacy even though the individual follower may not be proximate to the leader in any real sense. "Each individual within the charismatizing group feels a personal relationship with the leader—even if he has never met the leader."[14]

Naturally, chief executive officers must make their presence felt within their institutions in order to be effective. However, to be charismatic leaders they must transcend the bureaucratic structure and develop relationships with each manager and employee. Thomas Peters and Robert Waterman spoke of this type of management in their section on Hands-On Management. United Airlines' former head, Edward Carlson, attributed his turnaround of that company to the fact that "I travelled about 200,000 miles a year to express my concern for what I call 'visible management.' . . . I felt as though I were running for public office. . . . I wanted these people to identify [with] me."[15]

Oratory

If the various characteristics and/or attributes of the charismatic personality were to be prioritized, oratorical brilliance would rank at the top of the list. "Great and passionate oratory is one of the key ways in which charisma can be generated by a leader. The intersubjective communication of oratorical language can create a spell in which humans can become swayed and charismatically linked to a leader."[16]

Oratorical brilliance is the vehicle charismatic leaders use to excite their followers and impart their message. Through the use of their voices and of imagery in their speech, charismatic managers can create excitement within the work environment and stimulate employees to achieve greater productivity and higher quality because they, too, share the dream.

Vision

Charismatic leaders must have vision. They must be individuals who can see beyond the realities of the day and take quantum leaps into the future. Charismatic leaders, by definition, are people on a mission. They also operate by a value system and act consistently within the context of those values. Their values become deeply ingrained in the philosophy of the charismatic group and drive the group's goals.

Peters and Waterman found the excellent companies they reviewed all concentrated on just a few basic values:

> First . . . these values are almost always stated in qualitative, rather than quantitative, terms. . . .   A second attribute of effective value systems is the effort to inspire the people at the very

bottom of the organization. . . . While the most viable beliefs are soaring in one way or another, many merely emphasize the details of execution but in a fervent way.[17]

It is interesting to note that the value systems in these excellent companies were directed at fervently inspiring people. This sounds very much like the effect that charismatic leaders have on their communities.

Self-Confidence

Characteristics universally associated with charismatic leaders are their self-confidence and inner determination. "Charles de Gaulle epitomized this feature of complete confidence in the correctness of his position and in his capabilities to solve whatever was troubling France. Charismatics make this a clear aspect of their public image."[18] As long as the leaders are certain of the correctness of their mission, they can demand the loyalty of their followers. In fact, they inspire those they lead to overcome their fears with their own sustained resolve and confidence.

HOW CHARISMA IS ACQUIRED

Charisma is a radical concept, considering the traditional rigidities of most business organizational forms. However, with today's temporary systems and organic forms of organization, there may be room for this type of innovation and radical departure from the normative order. Apparently the excellent companies have employed some of these concepts in their institutions to achieve their success.

It is leaders' responsibility, as chief executive officers, to be the catalysts for change within their organizations. They should provide a vision and consistent value system that all members of their staffs can "buy into." This vision and value system must be communicated to all employees. Well-written and well-delivered speeches pack a greater emotional wallop than a letter or policy.

CEOs should give employees the illusion of being there with them. A President's Round Table can be set up to give employees the opportunity to see and talk with their CEO. Executives must make their presence felt. At all times, they must exude the greatest confidence in themselves and in the correctness of the direction the organization is taking. The appearance of inner determination may be the difference between staying the course or giving up the ship.

NOTES

1. Kojiro Miyahara, "Charisma from Weber to Contemporary Sociology," *Social Inquiry* 53 (Fall 1983):369.

2. S.N. Eisenstadt, *Max Weber on Charisma and Institution Building* (Chicago: University of Chicago Press, 1968):20.

3. Alan C. Filley, Robert J. House, and Stephen Kerr, *Managerial Process and Organizational Behavior* (Glenview, Ill.: Scott, Foresman & Company, 1976):92.

4. Filley, House, and Kerr, *Managerial Process,* 93.

5. Daniel Katz and Robert L. Kahn, *The Social Psychology of Organizations* (New York: John Wiley & Sons, Inc., 1966):220.

6. Miyahara, "Charisma," 370.

7. Liah Greenfeld, "Reflections on Two Charismas," *The British Journal of Sociology* 36 (March 1985):119.

8. Eisenstadt, *Max Weber,* 49–50.

9. Stephen Sharot, "Hasidism and the Routinization of Charisma," *Journal for the Scientific Study of Religion* 19 (December 1980):326–27.

10. Eisenstadt, *Max Weber,* 57.

11. Ibid.

12. Miyahara, "Charisma," 372.

13. Ronald Glassman, "Legitimacy and Manufactured Charisma," *Social Research* 42, no. 4 (Winter 1975): 616.

14. Ibid., 623.

15. Thomas Peters and Robert Waterman, *In Search of Excellence* (New York: Warner Books Inc., 1985):289–90.

16. Glassman, "Legitimacy," 630.

17. Peters and Waterman, *Search,* 284–85.

18. Bernard Bass, *Leadership and Performance Beyond Expectations* (New York: The Free Press, 1985): 45.

Leadership vs. Management: What's the Difference?

Austin Ross

2

Are executives born with leadership skills or are these skills acquired? Can a leader instinctively recognize these skills in others? What motivates an executive to move into a pattern of leadership? Do leadership skills really differ from managerial skills?

This chapter explores several of these issues. As with any analysis of leadership and management, conclusions should be challenged since these organizational patterns may well reflect exercises in art rather than technology or science. Observations based on experience, intuition, and opinion come into play in addressing leadership and management.

Harold Geneen, former chairman of ITT, states emphatically that "leadership cannot really be taught, it can only be learned."[1] Harold J. Leavitt, director of the Executive Program in the Graduate School of Business at Stanford University, suggests to the contrary that pathfinders (leaders) can indeed be taught, but it has to be worked at, and "we'll have to modify our regular definition of teaching to do so."[2]

MANAGEMENT: PAST AND PRESENT

Professional management surfaced in the early 1900s. Early structures were simpler. The boss/executive was readily identified. As society expanded, the ever-increasing enhancement of technology required more organizational structure. Succeeding generations of executives experienced these eras:

1. Initial organization and structure (1910–1935): This was an era of the growth of new industries and of entrepreneurship. It was an era of preregulation and high risk. The health industry was in its organiza-

tional infancy. Physicians were individual entrepreneurs and proud of it. Group practice was limited to a few Mayo-type structures that were in themselves controversial.

2. Productivity era (1935–1955): A "science" of management began to develop. Things were measured. Units were counted and factories mechanized. World War II had a profound impact on the organization of medicine and how it was delivered. The concept of integrated hospital care matured, and practitioners increasingly focused their activities close to the hospital setting.

3. Systems movement and management control (1955–1970): Technology continued to advance, and society responded with an endless appetite and a new expectation that medicine and the health system could continue to deliver quality care in limitless quantities. Within hospitals, management engineers were employed to further operational effectiveness. The new organizational charts stressed accountability and the differences between line and staff functions. Planning processes became formalized and structured.

4. System networking (1970–1980): Networking and linkages among hospitals, group practices, and other providers, developed initially to share resources and services, took on more importance as the regulation of the health industry began to limit decision-making flexibility. Organizations also began to appreciate that the public's expectation of unlimited access to medical care could not be met and that there were advantages in joining forces in order to achieve economies of scale and mutual protection. For-profit hospital systems began to flourish, existing nonprofit systems adopted more of a corporate structure and outlook, and independent institutions formed new alliances and consortia.

5. The new competition (1980 to current): This is the era of the shakeout and survival of the fittest. High technology, high expectations, and high costs have been the drivers for change. Competition is testing the traditional organizational climate. Health care entities are responding predictably, similar to other industries that experienced deregulation and competition. Hospital leaders are learning how to downsize operations, how to diversify to protect revenue bases, and how to rebuild management teams to contend with the need for more rapid decision making. In response to these external and internal pressures, organizations thrash around to create tighter internal control mechanisms while simultaneously seeking ways to reward risk takers and innovators. This internal conflict in management direction—as to whether to increase bureaucratic control or liberate the decision-making pro-

cesses—stresses the traditional management team and tests the organization's ability to implement crucial change processes.

MANAGEMENT: THE FUTURE

In the future, management styles will continue to reflect a response to the economic competition. Management theorists will discuss and assess how leaders are coping with an era involving the politics of subtraction. Organizations will look for ways to trim down management structures. Top-down bureaucratic control systems will be replaced by focused management teams. The art of blending management specialties into highly integrated and interdependent teams will become even more essential.

An age of executive excellence will focus on this organizational integration and renewal. CEOs previously focused on refining managerial skills, but tomorrow they will spend more time identifying and rewarding individuals who are risk takers with innovation and vision rather than institutional caretakers.

LEADERSHIP CULTURE

Stanford's Leavitt suggests that organizations include three basic types of manager/leader: the implementors, the problem identifiers, and the pathfinders.[3]

Implementors are on the firing line. They have the task of convincing subordinates of the need to accomplish specific objectives. Implementors deal with all of the emotional factors associated with making things happen. They also must live with the consequences of their actions.

Problem identifiers are those who are endowed with analytical skills. They know how to confront issues and make a case for change. Problem identifiers also tend to be impatient with those responsible for implementing change.

Pathfinders are visionaries who peer over the horizon. Pathfinders can be inconsistent since, at times, they downplay or even ignore facts and rely heavily on intuition. However, they provide organizational balance to the managerial process. They also tend to focus on "mission" as being a crucial factor in making decisions. Leaders and managers, of course, assume these roles interchangeably.

CEOs, interested in team building, should keep these characteristics in mind. The organizations that will prosper in the future may well be those whose leaders have learned how to maintain this balance of implementation, problem identification, and pathfinding.

HIGH-PERFORMING HEALTH CARE ORGANIZATIONS

Stephen Shortell of Northwestern University suggests some classic characteristics may be found in high-performing health care organizations in the 1980s. He suggests that these characteristics include a willingness and ability to:

1. stretch themselves
2. maximize learning
3. take risks
4. exhibit transforming leadership
5. exercise a bias for action
6. create a chemistry among top leaders
7. manage ambiguity and uncertainty
8. exhibit a "loose coherence"
9. exhibit a well-defined culture
10. reflect a basic spirituality.[4]

Shortell's characteristics stress interpersonal relationship skills rather than accountability and highly defined structure. The characteristics do not seem to focus on a careful delineation between line and staff functions or highly defined organizational relationships. While Shortell does not diminish the need for solid management direction, he implies that high-performing health care organizations seem to take it for granted that good management is in place. These organizations look for ways to motivate individuals to take risks and be innovative and creative, then to reward them for such behavior.

LEADERS OR MANAGERS?

Do leaders really function differently from managers? For example, do leaders delegate differently? Are managers more constrained to operate in terms of tight control and performance? Are leaders equally concerned with controls and performance or do they move from a focus on immediate problems to the larger picture? Do they move more easily from the present-day tactics to longer range strategy? Do leaders roll more easily with the punches? Are short-range gains sacrificed to achieve longer range goals? Do leaders deal more easily with uncertainty and ambiguity?

In relation to investing in the future, do managers tend to focus on coping with today's budget while leaders, when confronted with the same set of circumstances, examine the immediate problem of resource allocation but also peer over the horizon to see how today's decision bears on the future?

Leaders, of course, cope with creative tension. It may be easier to contend with facts and certainty (and shorter range conclusions) than with ambiguity and uncertainty. The ability of leaders to deal with this uncertainty over time may be a point of difference between managing and leading.

Both leaders and managers are deeply involved in solving interpersonal relationships. The method and/or degree of control used may relate to the educational and experiential background of the individual. Students exposed to only one management model initially may base their management style on what they have learned in the past. Those with a wider base of experience may approach control issues differently through the use of a variety of solutions to address specific problems. The extent of control used by the executives also tells much about their perception of trust.

Generalities about management control issues are hazardous. There are times when decisive management behavior, with a minimum of consensus building, is the preferred approach. This occurs when the organization faces the need for tight timelines in decision making. Activities then have to be closely controlled and quickly implemented.

The Marine Corps lieutenant in command of a platoon in combat must be a leader, but that is a time for command decisions, not consensus. The extent of control exercised also varies according to the capacity of members of the management team to make (and accept) decisions. The leaders are responsible for assessing the competency of subordinates. Less experienced managers may require more direction and control than do more experienced ones. Every individual comes equipped with a different set of experiences and complicates any process that attempts to differentiate control in a context of leading or managing.

But managers probably do approach control issues differently from leaders. Managers work harder to create structure and, to develop order and progress, they build practices based on precedence and policies. Leaders probably relate more to the complexity of an issue and place a value on maintaining "wiggle" room to allow flexible approaches to those difficult problems. Leaders function more by managing by exception than by managing by policy and precedence.

MANAGERIAL PRACTICES

Management theories (X, Y, and more recently Z), the past and current descriptions relating to management styles, contribute to the leader/manager dilemma. The adoption of a concept of management by objective (MBO) to set operating goals probably has frustrated more leaders and managers than any other technique.

The weakness in implementing an MBO process surfaces in the second or third levels of an organization. Too frequently these managers are poorly equipped to set measurable goals, since tradition dictates that goal setting starts only at the top. To further complicate the picture, the competency of first-line supervisors varies immensely. Coping with these variables requires that executives invest tremendous time and effort. As a result, many chief executive officers who instituted an MBO program were disappointed with the end result and many such programs were abandoned.

As each new generation of administrators appreciated the importance of involving subordinates in the process of setting quantitatively oriented objectives, another theory surfaced that preached the virtues of freewheeling decision making and the need to take organizational risks.

The socialization of management processes designed to create a lasting corporate culture contributes another dimension to an already complex picture. Corporate culture relates to the processes that the organization and its leaders use to instill in individuals a sense of tradition, worth, and value. The focus of the cultural socialization process is to persuade each individual to buy into the organization and to transmit to others this sense of special purpose or dedication to a specific corporate cause. The creation of a corporate culture requires leadership based on sensitivity and trust.

In terms of building a culture, leaders focus first on the environment, identify organizational strengths and weaknesses, and create a team to meet current and future needs. Managers, however, may address organizational culture more personally, based on experiences that have succeeded or failed in the past. Managers rely on what has worked before. This focus on the environment, as contrasted with a focus on past experience, may help differentiate leaders from managers.

Another exercise that tests managers and leaders relates to planning. Strategic planning involves the expenditure of effort to define the organization's mission, collect data to identify trends, and then to project all this into the future. Countless meetings among planners, administrators, board members, and physicians are required. Good strategic planning suggests the need for close interrelations between the planners and the executives.

THE IMPORTANCE OF BALANCE

The leader often becomes uncomfortable with the required technical methodology of planning and seeks shortcuts to hasten the process. On the other hand, managers may focus on the planning process and thereby, risk missing larger strategic implications. Leaders know that planning is important to focus direction and resources but may miss the target by leaping to conclusions. Good planning requires the skills of both leaders and managers.

Identifying the characteristics by which managers and leaders approach similar tasks is important to executives interested in building the strongest possible team. Team leaders must attract individuals who will contribute balance to the managerial processes.

The balance often is very fragile. Leaders must perpetually fine-tune the team to meet the changes in the internal and external environment. Team leaders mentor well and teach. They also have the courage to make changes if required. Leaders know the importance of protecting organizational values and of coping with temporary setbacks and failure.

Team leaders appreciate the critical nature of continuing education, for themselves and for their subordinates. Risk taking also is important, and the leaders know instinctively that team members must be encouraged to take risks or the momentum of the organization will be lost.

Reflecting on these subtle differences between leading and managing is of importance if great management teams are to be assembled and sustained. If there is a single factor or key that differentiates leaders from managers, it must lie in the executives' level of self-awareness.

EXECUTIVE RESPONSIBILITY

The manner in which leaders execute responsibility varies according to their individual style and specialty. How managers or leaders perceive responsibility may account for additional differences as to how assignments are executed. The organizational environment, its economic well-being and extent or lack of growth also are powerful forces in determining how the executives will respond in performing administrative functions.

One means of focusing on the subtle differences between leaders and managers is to hypothesize as to how each would address functional assignments.

Table 2-1 identifies assignments, then predicts a probable response of the leader and the manager. As noted earlier, leaders function as managers and managers function as leaders, depending on the circumstances and the nature of the situation. It is useful, however, to examine these characteristics as one means of identifying where on a continuum an individual might be placed—at that moment or point in time.

Table 2-1 Responses to Executive Assignments

Assignment	Manager Response	Leader Response
Time management	Focus: daily events	Focus: project or goal
Planning	Tactical, incident oriented	Strategic, continual
Values	Accepted, supported	Developed, expanded
Risk taking	Defined limits	Flexible limits
Management succession planning	Reactive, based on current need	Proactive, based on future need
Delegating	Prescriptive	Flexible
Span of control	Carefully defined vertical structure	Matrix oriented and fluid
Follow-up	Detailed and tight	Variable, based on perceived need
Disciplining	Personal and direct	More subtle and indirect
Team building	Goal directed	Strategic in scope
Accepting failure	Introverted and self-critical	Tendency to rationalize and rebound
Mentoring	Transfer of technical skill	Transfer of knowledge

THE IMPORTANCE OF SELF-AWARENESS

There are a number of techniques to help develop self-awareness and contribute to the process of strengthening leadership skills:

- Self-assessment. This refers to a process executives use to identify strengths and weaknesses. The American College of Healthcare Executives' Self-Assessment Program is an example of an objective self-testing skill evaluation process that helps individuals track competency over time.
- Intuitive skills. Leaders understand that organizational goals are achieved through processes that encourage personal commitment. It is the leaders' ability to identify others willing to commit to a cause that contributes to the growth of great management teams. Intuition and vision materially help this process. Intuitive skills can be strengthened if the individuals are aware of their importance and use. Intuitive skills can be acquired, if not inherited, but must be worked, tested, and used to achieve awareness.
- Sensitivity and feedback. A directive manager translates command into action and directs subordinates to meet that goal. The manager requires information feedback to measure the level of accomplishment. Leaders, too, depend on feedback to measure the level of accomplishment

or failure but may approach the feedback process more randomly. They place follow-up priorities on monitoring exceptions or unusual events rather than on expected and normal occurrences. This is referred to as management by exception. The means by which feedback is obtained may help differentiate managing from leading.

- Knowledge of self. This is a fundamental characteristic of leadership. A number of superb leaders seem to have some degree of insecurity rather than overdeveloped egos (although this insecurity may be well concealed). This works to the leaders' advantage because it reminds them that they are fallible. This insecurity also conditions them to their environment. Knowledge of self permits a certain level of personal detachment. Circumstances and issues can be analyzed more easily and unemotionally, allowing for longer range rational approaches to tough decisions.

SPECIFIC STRATEGIES

Discrete leadership formulas cannot be tacked to an office wall and used. Leadership strategy encompasses a substantial degree of artistry. Leadership is a fluctuating, high-tech, high-touch activity. Different styles are used to cope with different situations.

Executives need to specify leadership strategies early and to recognize that they will change with time. The development of external factors such as competition in the health care industry suggests that new strategies are needed. In turn, internal factors also affect these strategies.

In earlier days, management structures were defined in tightknit organizational charts; today, they are fluid and flexible.

There also are factors that change with less speed and need to be monitored very closely. These include:

- Value systems. These are critical components of leadership. Followers look closely for value statements from their leaders. Value systems ensure personal credibility, trust, and integrity. If the leader is not willing to articulate values and live by them, members of the team will be distrustful. One example of a value system in the organization relates to the method the team leader uses to communicate to team members the means by which they can confront each other when opinions differ. The value is that confrontation is encouraged (because it is inappropriate to have team members operating in a setting of groupthink), but confrontations must be open and respectful of others' integrity.

- Ethics. Value systems and ethics are interrelated. To codify ethics for a professional society is highly appropriate and serves to provide guideposts along the way. But leaders translate broader ethical issues into the day-to-day operation by knowing the difference between right and wrong and by setting the example. Because of the complexity of issues, decisions are often cast in shades of gray. Lines are not always clear. Leaders often make decisions by applying a fundamental test of "is it right or wrong" in order to clarify issues for the team and for the organization.

To develop their own personal leadership strategies, executives first must learn about themselves. This includes developing team feedback, perpetuating a personal program of self-assessment (including a comparison with peers), and allocating enough time to think and reflect about issues.

They must learn as much as possible about those with whom they associate in order to know how they operate and function, including identification of their strengths and weaknesses. Executives then match their strengths and weaknesses with those of these associates. The result is that the team output is improved and synergistic.

Executives must pay close attention to the organizational culture. It takes time to build culture, and those who work in an entity that has a strong culture must take great care to protect and preserve it. In a new organization or one with a culture in disarray, a high priority for the leader is to nudge the entity to identify (or create) its culture.

It is essential to know the organization's mission and how to tinker with the mission, if necessary, to move programs forward.

Leaders must know the environment, how their competition operates, and how they measure against that competition.

Personal development must be emphasized. Leaders must truly "read and write" throughout their career. This ability must not be left behind in the classroom. Leaders also become involved in activities beyond those defined in the organizational chart by participating in professional and community endeavors. These additional activities provide the essential balance that leaders need.

And finally, associating with strong leaders and networking provides executives with crucial input. Leaders at all levels in the organization should be encouraged to network for personal and professional reasons.

THE KEYS TO LEADERSHIP

Differences between leading and managing have been discussed. Successful leaders control the energy that goes into managing and leading.

Differentiating between leadership and management is useful only as a means of encouraging individuals to develop introspection about their career development.

Leadership is the conscious state of awareness of how individuals can affect an organization's change process. It is the means by which they consciously apply themselves to determining direction and course. It is the understanding of skills and style and their application to a course of action. It is the consolidation of various activities to determine direction.

As noted earlier, leadership strategies are influenced by a continually changing environment, so they are not static. They always involve a certain risk, and risk sometimes leads to failure, so in developing such activities, executives must be prepared to cope with some failure.

Leadership strategies also are affected by organizational scale. The complexity of health systems requires organization in order to integrate and focus effort. But there is a major difference between leadership involved in developing a productive, benevolent, innovative bureaucracy and one based on a tyranny of spirit and responsive only to tight autocratic control.

Leadership obviously is a personal event. While strategies may be based on acquired skills, the volatility of the environment, including the unpredictable nature of the impact on others, clearly places the design of those strategies in the grouping of art, not science.

It is unimportant whether leaders are born or made, since the obvious answer is that they are neither. Executives lead with different styles; there is no single successful model to follow. Most leaders simply work harder at doing what they do best and, by so doing, move themselves and others to new levels of activity and achievement.

If there is one fundamental characteristic of what contributes to the maintenance of leaders, it is their commitment to a lifelong process of learning, both on and off the job. It is a process of surpassing barriers, imposed by self or by others, that inhibit the receptivity of new knowledge.

Leaders are those who seek the means of translating existing facts and information into something new and different—perhaps a new and better way of doing something, or an element that contributes to an expanded program, or a better way of solving an existing problem.

Leaders are always learning, always seeking new information. They read materials such as books and journals, but most particularly they learn early how to read people. The leaders' tools are based on solid, tested management practices but these tools must be applied with sensitivity and purpose and adjusted to meet current conditions and needs.

The question of whether executives are leaders or follower/managers really is irrelevant, since in the larger scope of things true leadership requires both an awareness of managerial techniques and how they are best applied, and the instinct to motivate, to challenge, and to inspire others to achieve and succeed.

The ultimate test of leadership, then, is whether individuals possess the sensitivity to recognize how they fit into the organizational framework and, even more fundamentally, whether their role provides that particular and special sense of satisfaction of knowing that leading is worth the effort and energy required to make the difference.

NOTES

1. Harold Geneen, with Alvin Moscow, *Managing* (Garden City, N.Y.: Doubleday & Co., Inc., 1984):127.

2. Harold J. Leavitt, *Corporate Pathfinders* (Homewood, Ill: Dow Jones-Irwin, 1986):79.

3. Leavitt, *Corporate Pathfinders,* 2–14.

4. Stephen Shortell, "High Performing Healthcare Organizations: Guidelines for the Pursuit of Excellence," *Hospital & Health Services Administration* 30, no. 4 (July/August 1985):7.

Peak Performance Psychology

William C. Mason and J. Larry Read

3

People often feel that their future will be much like what happened today—mostly the same, just bigger, faster, and more or less of it. However, in recent years the lessons of the energy crunch, irreversible environmental damage, and innovative space technology have begun to make the point: the future will be very different from today.

The same can be said of the health care industry. With prospective reimbursement, technological advances, declining inpatient census, patient demand shifts to outpatient modes of treatment, and the proliferation of alternative delivery systems, the health care industry is changing. Its future, too, thus will be quite different from today.

These dramatic evolutions are changing the role, the expectations, and the outcomes of health care institutions. These changes have resulted in new challenges for chief executive officers and the management team: increasing institutional productivity; meeting challenges in the marketplace; evaluating advances in technology; maximizing reimbursement schemes; and educating the governing board, medical staff, employees, and consumers about these changes. In this time of rapid change, chief executive officers also are evaluating their role, management style and techniques, and productivity in order to meet these challenges.

CHANGES FROM BEING "JUST HOSPITALS"

The time has passed when health care institutions can be considered "just hospitals." The changing external environment has increased their scope and complexity. With the proliferation of alternative delivery systems and greater competition among all health care providers, hospitals are employing a variety of marketing techniques, many for the first time, in their

31

efforts to increase or maintain market share in a declining marketplace. These techniques include marketing research to differentiate among their actual or prospective consumer groups, to ascertain perceived needs of those groups, and to identify niches for the institutions, as well as advertising their services/products in the mass media.

Existing and proposed changes in the reimbursement philosophy and mechanisms of the federal government, together with increasing competition among providers for health care dollars, have caused these organizations to reexamine their services and procedures. The eroding inpatient census, the increasing emphasis on ambulatory services, and the emergence of prospective reimbursement have caused institutions to reevaluate their modus operandi and to increase productivity and efficiency in all areas, thus reducing overall costs. This shift has resulted in the redefining of programs and the further development of alternative outpatient services. This horizontally integrated growth has generated a need for different technology, reimbursement, financial considerations, mindset, and skills to manage these new enterprises.

The interface with the medical staff is changing. The medical staff is the customer of the institution, a relationship that is being further fostered by a number of institutions that support and attempt to enhance the medical practice of individual providers through innovative marketing ideas and techniques. In addition, a number of alternative health care ventures are being developed that provide entrepreneurial opportunities for physicians; some of these are joint endeavors with the hospital, others are commercial operations. These can provide a much closer relationship with physicians in the institution as well as opportunities to compete for patients and dollars (commercial ventures).

In this rapidly changing environment, chief executive officers are challenged, not only to remain out in front of these changes and to plot an appropriate course of action but also to educate their major constituents. Keeping the governing board, the medical staff, and the management team educated as to the rapidly changing environment is a must.

The new challenges and opportunities have resulted in new demands on the CEOs' time and have created a need for attaining new levels of personal productivity over a long period, much like the world-class hurdler Edwin Moses, who won more than 100 consecutive races. This new level must be sustained, in contrast to periodic peaking and subsequent return to previous levels.

This chapter outlines the characteristics of peak performers and of techniques that may be utilized to produce continually at high levels. These techniques, applicable to those in both athletics and in business, are not new but are athletic theorems restated for business management. This process calls for a better definition and visualization of the anticipated level of performance, a commitment to its accomplishment, a narrowing of outside distractions, and a mental rehearsal of all steps before execution. The result is more relaxed, confident, prepared individuals who are anticipating the upcoming "performance."

THE MISSION

It has been said that people can take any road when they are not sure where they want to go. This cannot be said of peak performers. They have a defined direction—a mission. Just as a well-defined mission statement gives direction to a corporation, this direction is used by the peak performers to guide their future actions. The mission reflects the individuals' overall basic philosophies, values, and priorities and broadly frames intentions and actions. Such passionate belief and direction establish a basis for the setting of goals so that all energies and resources can be directed toward the desired outcome.

Peak performers are characterized as proactive, self-disciplined, enthusiastic, tenacious individuals who are driven by a desire for, and a clear expectation of, success.

Abraham Maslow called persons who assume control of their mental and physical skills in order to perform optimally on a consistent basis "self-actualizing people." These individuals need to realize their capabilities and potentials through achieving very high, definite goals.[1] The first step is to focus completely on self, assuming active responsibility and accountability for all actions and resulting outcomes. This is the key to the process and results in individuals taking charge of their lives. Self-actualizing individuals initiate activities that are planned toward accomplishing their goals rather than merely responding to external circumstances. By taking the initiative, peak performers can make their own choices rather than selecting from the external alternatives presented at random. By knowing the intended outcomes, peak performers can sort through their alternatives, consider the potential obstacles in their path, plan their strategy, and proceed in a positive, confident manner.

Proactive performers are self-starters. Their action attitude is that if a person is to climb a mountain, the first movement starts by moving oneself. Such individuals are driven so, in addition to initiating a project, they actively work toward its completion. They believe that whatever is to happen can be controlled by their actions, first through knowing the desired result and secondly through meticulously self-developed plans and actions.

Dr. Norman Vincent Peale was asked, "What is the greatest word in the English language?" He answered that, based on the Bible, the greatest words in the English language are love, hope, and faith.[2] Outside the Bible, he said, the greatest word is enthusiasm. Peale observes that the people who accomplish the most in this world are those who are filled with a driving enthusiasm. He believes that the world belongs to enthusiasts who can keep their cool and at the same time have a terrific, driving energy. Peale describes enthusiasts as those who love the world, love life, love their job, love people, and can't wait until the next morning so they can get to work again. Peak performers—enthusiasts—believe that what will happen in the future can be determined by their influence, choices, and actions, and they feel a sense of urgency to accomplish their mission.

Two other primary characteristics of a peak performer are perseverance and self-discipline. President Calvin Coolidge wrote:

> Nothing in the world can take the place of perseverance. Talent will not; nothing is more common than unsuccessful men with talent. Genius will not; unrewarded genius is almost a proverb. Education will not; the world is full of educated derelicts. Persistence and determination alone are omnipotent.[3]

Self-discipline in individuals denotes tenacity or stick-to-itiveness. It involves a discipline to strive consistently for the desired goals. It also denotes a constant commitment to disregard the many external factors that would detract from the work to be accomplished. This commitment is demonstrated by many athletes as they prepare for major events. Many know of Bruce Jenner's training commitment for the 1976 Olympiad and can name others who, for a specific period, have made the total commitment to a particular athletic endeavor. While relatively few people ever will train for such an event or have the luxury of making such a total commitment of time and effort, the principle remains the same. Peak performers have a passionate drive to accomplish a goal or goals and are willing to say no to external factors that would detract them from their commitment. The peak performers assume active responsibility for their actions and their nonactions.

Typically, individuals can improve their overall performance through periodic evaluation of their management of time. This can be as simple as improving the method of utilizing the telephone, delegating projects to subordinates, or making sure that time spent on projects is consistent with the goals. Often, better time management will provide for a maximization of the hours allocated to a specific project or goal, with a resulting benefit of free time for leisure.

THE GOALS

In his book *Peak Performance,* Charles A. Garfield describes a unique characteristic exhibited in peak performers that he calls volition.[4] This characteristic manifests itself in a variety of ways: as a passionate desire for success, a feeling of "I will do it," or a commitment to oneself to accomplish something important. Garfield draws the analogy of volition to electric energy, suggesting that electricity offers only a potential until it is harnessed and guided to an appropriate device. Volition is the inner energy that causes individuals to be driven in one direction. Volition may be described as single-mindedness, determination, drive, and an overarching desire to fulfill personal goals.

In *See You at the Top,* Zig Ziglar describes this same force as desire.[5] He believes that desire is the ingredient that makes the difference between an average performer and a champion. The champion has a great desire to accomplish personal goals, to make a difference. The peak performer has a vaulting ambition, a zeal for accomplishment. This inner force, although intangible, can be "seen" in the confidence and concentration exhibited by peak performers.

Garfield attempts to synthesize the best sports research conducted in the United States, the Soviet Union, East Germany, and elsewhere into a result-oriented self-development program for athletic endeavors.[6] He says all athletic accomplishments begin with volition—a desire, a willpower necessary to succeed. He adds that volition affects physical performance, as well as thoughts and feelings about the performance. It has been shown that strength, responsiveness, stamina, and precision of movement all can be influenced by volition.

Based on the broad framework (mission), plus the volition for accomplishment, the next step is to define the mission in terms of the specific goals to be accomplished. While the mission and goals are closely allied, each stands alone and deserves attention. Peak performers are motivated by a deep and personal sense of mission that broadly defines their philosophy, values, and priorities. However, it is necessary to reduce this broad thrust to smaller, specific, and measurable goals. These serve as major stepping stones toward the eventual expression and actualization of the mission.

The goals are distinctly different from the mission in that they are highly specific and measurable. Since a mission is personal and subjective, it is distinguished from a goal in that the goal is an objective statement about a specific achievement that can be measured quantitatively. Each goal should be thought out clearly and each should have a timetable for initiation and completion. The development and definition of a number of goals is necessary to realize the actualization of the desired mission.

The first step in developing the goal(s) is to define what is to be accomplished in the future. What are the desired outcomes? Looking into the future is difficult because it is unknown. However, it is important to push into the future in dreaming and planning so that the process of developing goals is not limited by memories of the past. Individuals should aspire not simply to repeat a prior performance level but to reach a new and higher level. While they can learn from past experiences, it is imperative that they push into the future and raise the level of expectations. It is only through this process of stretching the imagination that the desired level of peak performance can be anticipated, visualized, and realized. Therefore, the first step is to stretch the imagination into the future and carefully define what is to be accomplished.

Focusing on these aspirations forces contemplation of a number of options and alternative performance levels. The preferred options must be selected from among the various alternatives. As a result of this narrowing, the preferred future expectations become clear and a course to reach actualization can be plotted. Effective goal setting begins with today's status and focuses on the desired future status. From these two reference points, present and future, a blueprint can be developed for the systematic achievement of the goals. The technique of divide and conquer is used so that the quantitative and time-limited goals can be subdivided into a series of smaller steps, each with a high probability of achievement. These incremental points, often called action steps, should be both quantitatively measurable and time limited.

One of the keys in developing the incremental steps of the long-term goal is to define carefully the level of expectations of each incremental step. The scope of activity in each step should be considered and, as noted, each should have a high probability of achievement. The incremental steps must be sufficiently challenging or motivation will be destroyed. Conversely, if they are too challenging, the task may seem overwhelming and, again, motivation can be destroyed. It is necessary to assess each goal to ensure that each incremental step not only is challenging but also has a high probability of accomplishment.

The final element in goal setting is the creation of mental images of the desired outcomes. These images are made first of the mission and, subsequently, of each goal and each incremental action step. With the goals clearly visualized as mental images, the individuals will have a mental model for the desired action steps, performance level, and eventual outcome.

THE FUNCTION OF IMAGING

Peale said one of the greatest mental techniques known to man is imaging.[7] In the goal-setting process, imaging is used for visualizing the goal and each of the incremental steps.

Imaging is defined by Webster as the "process of forming a mental picture of something not yet actually present." Einstein said the most important thing a person can have is knowledge and the second most important is the creative ability of imagination.[8] He believed that without imagination, knowledge is devoid of power.

In recent years, one of the most dramatic contributions to the advancement of goal-setting skills has been the introduction of visualization by the Soviets.[9] Soviet athletes use this process extensively in improving their individual skills. Visualization, as defined by the Soviets, is the refinement of mental rehearsal techniques that allows individuals to create mental images of the exact movements they want to emulate in accomplishing their goals. As stated previously, the first step is knowing exactly what is to be accomplished and the second is defining the incremental steps.

The Soviet athletes identify every movement necessary to accomplish the incremental steps and, thus, the goal. Each of the physical movements is calculated mentally in exact detail, then rehearsed. Combined with the theory of practice makes perfect, these mental images of action movements are rehearsed continually until they are ready for use. The results of these training endeavors are evidenced by the Soviets' performance in the 1976 Olympics, where they won more gold medals than any other country, and ever since have had world-class performers in virtually every athletic event.

A well-known major league baseball player has said that while still in the clubhouse before a game he studies each opposing pitcher and visualizes each pitch, and continues to do so in the on-deck circle during the game. He visualizes not only the motion of the pitcher and the rotation of the ball, but also his swing and the resulting base hit. After this preparation, he is confident and anticipates his time at bat, when he merely follows through on the images he developed in the clubhouse and in the on-deck circle.

One of golf's greatest players has said that he visualizes the outcome of each of his golf swings before he hits the ball. He mentally practices each part of his swing and follow-through several times first. The process also includes visualizing the route of the ball after it is hit, its bounce, and its eventual lie on the fairway or its pathway on the green. He uses this technique for every swing, whether he is on a practice tee or on the 18th hole at the Masters tournament.

This process of visualization, whether for an athletic endeavor or planning a business strategy, allows individuals to work out complex actions before they actually are executed. With a known outcome (goal), each of the alternatives can be evaluated independently and various scenarios can be developed and tested mentally. In this manner, the optimal steps to accomplish the goal are defined. Through mental rehearsal, the capabilities of the mind are used in a positive way by choosing the neurological patterns that will guide both the physical and mental movements. This choice of movements provides the opportunity for planning as well as rehearsing the necessary actions in a specific situation.

As Peale explains, "The image moves from your conscious mind into your subconscious mind through 'mental osmosis' and not only do you have it [the image] but it also has you."[10] Another advantage of this process of planning and rehearsal is that the possible alternatives and scenarios can be developed and analyzed in an objective and dispassionate manner. It has been said that the human mind works best when it is "cool" rather than when it is running "hot."[11] When the optimal scenario and moves are defined, as rehearsal implies, they may be practiced over and over before they are used in the "performance."

Once the necessary moves and skills are perfected through mental rehearsal, individuals are ready to perform. Whether in an athletic event or a meeting of the board of directors, they can be comfortable in their tasks because the extensive preparation produces a sense of confidence from being well prepared to handle the situation. The executives will have an inner sense of optimism and a newly found sense of control. They are prepared with the right moves to produce the intended results. This intense preparation will guide their actions in the event for which they have prepared; it also engenders an inner feeling of self-confidence before and during the event. This feeling, which is readily telegraphed, will be observed by the other participants. The sureness comes from the knowledge that each action has been well analyzed and practiced as steps toward accomplishing the goal. With this meticulous preparation, the level of confidence must be higher than it would be without such preparation.

Garfield reports eight characteristic feelings that are present in athletes when they are performing at their peak.[12] The athletes have feelings of being:

1. MENTALLY RELAXED. Of all the feeling states examined, a sense of inner calm is by far the most frequently mentioned. Along with this inner calm, athletes often report feeling a sense of time being slowed down and having a high degree of concentration. By contrast, a loss of concentration, a sense of everything happening too fast, and a sense of things being out of control are associated with mental tension.

2. PHYSICALLY RELAXED. A feeling that the muscles are loose, with movements fluid, precise, and sure, is closely linked with peak performance.

3. CONFIDENT AND OPTIMISTIC, WITH A GENERALLY POSITIVE OUTLOOK. A feeling of self-confidence, a positive attitude, or an inner sense of optimism about being able to perform well is reported as a key factor that determines whether the athlete can transform a potentially threatening athletic challenge into a success while maintaining poise.

4. FOCUSED ON THE PRESENT. Athletes report having a sense of mind-body integration or harmony between mental and physical functions, and having no thoughts or feelings about the past or future. (Learning to be "in the present" is one of the key disciplines taught in the martial arts.) When completely focused on the present, logical and analytical processes are suspended, and as this occurs the athlete has the sense that all actions are occurring automatically and effortlessly.

5. HIGHLY ENERGIZED. Words such as joy, ecstasy, intensity, and power are frequently used to describe this highly energized state. Although fear, anxiety, and even rage have been traditionally associated with high performance levels, these feelings were rarely mentioned as contributing in any way to this high energy state.

6. EXTRAORDINARY AWARENESS. Athletes almost universally describe a state of mind in which they are acutely aware of their bodies and of the athletes around them and have an uncanny ability to anticipate correctly other athletes' moves and respond effectively to them. This awareness is closely related to the state of being focused on the present (see 4, above).

7. IN CONTROL. Although athletes report a feeling of being in control, the control described is largely subconscious. There appears to be no deliberate effort at the moment of peak performance to exert control over the situations around them or over other people, but there is a definite sense of being able to make all the right moves, with the results being exactly what they intended.

8. IN THE "COCOON." The word cocoon has been used for many years to describe the sense of being insulated from the anxiety or fear ordinarily associated with particularly challenging athletic situations which would normally arouse fight-or-flight responses. Being in this cocoon, the athlete is able to avoid the loss of concentration, the accelerated, tight-muscled,

out-of-control feelings commonly associated with the fight-or-flight response.*

Peak performers thus are motivated by a deep and personal sense of mission and have identified what they want to accomplish in the changing future. The first step in the actualization of these dreams is to define the steppingstones (goals) that must be accomplished in order to obtain the intended outcomes. These goals must be defined in terms that are quantifiably measurable, time limited, and have a high probability of achievement. Second, each of the action steps and movements within each goal is planned, and through the process of visualization is continually rehearsed mentally until each action is perfected.

With this preparation, individuals' confidence and ability are enhanced, leading to a higher level of performance in a rapidly changing world.

NOTES

1. Edwin B. Flippo, *Management: A Behavioral Approach* (Boston: Allyn & Bacon, Inc., 1970), 90.

2. Speech delivered in Fort Worth, Texas, December 1977. Sound cassette.

3. Leonard Safir and William Safire, comps., *Good Advice* (New York: New York Times Books, 1982), 250.

4. Charles A. Garfield, with Hal Zina Bennett, *Peak Performance* (Los Angeles: Jeremy P. Tarcher, Inc., 1984), 33.

5. Zig Ziglar, *See You at the Top* (Gretna, La.: Pelican Publishing Company, 1980), 333.

6. Garfield and Bennett, *Peak Performance*, 2.

7. Speech delivered in Fort Worth, Texas, December 1977. Sound cassette.

8. Ibid.

9. Garfield and Bennett, *Peak Performance*, 127.

10. Speech delivered in Fort Worth, Texas, December 1977. Sound cassette.

11. Ibid.

12. Garfield and Bennett, *Peak Performance*, 158–60.

---

*Reprinted from *Peak Performance* by C.A. Garfield with H.Z. Bennett, pp. 158–160, with permission of Jeremy P. Tarcher, Inc., © 1984.

Effective Motivation

Ken W. Sargent and Arlene A. Sargent

4

"Explain to me about motivation," said the owner. "Does the coach provide motivation by telling the team to go out and win one for Max Zaslofsky? Does he say, 'Win this game, and I'll let you all stay up and watch the Johnny Carson Show the next time we're in Detroit?'"

"No," the General Manager said. "Motivation is a more subtle art. The coach has to make his players feel wanted. He has to make them feel they're contributing. He has to make them feel good."

The owner thought that over.

"The last time I looked at my books," he said, "I was paying about two and a half million dollars a season in salaries. Doesn't that make them feel wanted? Doesn't that make them feel good?"

"It would me," said the General Manager. "But times have changed. All that money simply makes our players self-satisfied. Big cash ties their legs together so they can't dive for loose balls, and turns their brains into fettucini so they can't figure out when to switch and when to play their own man."[1]

Times have indeed changed. For health care executives struggling to bring about organizational change and adaptation in a time of fundamental restructuring throughout the industry, two points seem paramount:

1. Managers must be motivated to unusual levels of risk taking, entrepreneurship, and change management at least until the early 1990s if sustainable organizational competitive advantage is to be achieved.
2. The "old rules" for effective motivation taught in undergraduate and graduate courses on management do not seem to work very well, at

least not in the context of the level of effort and commitment these times require. To put it another way, what is required now is particularly effective means of ensuring motivation, and Max Zaslofsky is nowhere in sight.

It should be added that such times also are times of unusual opportunity for both institutions and their managers; what is required is that they have the insight and discipline to respond to the opportunities presented. Effective response must be not from the individual but rather from teams of people working together to bring about focused organizational effort.

THE MOTIVATION PROBLEM

How can managers motivate others to such achievement? The dictionary defines motivation as the act or process of motivating. The root word, motive, is defined as a "psychological need or similar impulse acting as an incitement to action." For purposes here, motivation could be defined as the sum total of the influences that result in some action of the individual. The search for the principles of effective motivation should begin with the recognition that motives come from within the individual and are unique to each person, given their uniqueness as people.

Management is an old business. For thousands of years members of the human race have organized themselves to accomplish certain tasks and assigned responsibility to bring about such organization to selected members of their number. However, only within parts of the last century were the processes of management and the advantages and disadvantages of forms of organization studied systematically. Even more recent have been efforts to understand the nature of human beings and the processes of motivation within management. Perhaps only in the last two decades has there been a real urgency in this regard, stimulated by a heightened awareness of the general dissatisfaction of large numbers of people with their work lives.

Yankelovich reports that "In the decade between the late 1960s and the late 1970s, the number of Americans who believe 'hard work always pays off' fell from a 58 percent majority to a 43 percent minority."[2] For those in health care, that dissatisfaction is expressing itself in poor productivity, waste of resources, absenteeism, turnover, and ultimately the delivery of substandard patient care.

If health care institutions are to maximize their effectiveness in delivering patient care, it can only be in the context of a recognition that they must begin maximizing the use of their most critical resource—the human one. That can be accomplished by understanding how health care professionals function and what assumptions managers have made about human nature and motivation, since it is these assumptions that form the underlying basis for managerial action directed toward motivation.

A comprehensive review of organizational psychology is beyond the scope of this chapter; purposes here can best be served through a summary review of the tenets of three of the major historical contributors to the literature—Douglas McGregor, Abraham Maslow, and Frederick Herzberg—and an extrapolation of these principles into the environmental situation in health care.

THE THEORY X IMPACT

As noted previously, until very recently there had been little investigation into the nature of people in the workplace. McGregor summarized cogently the traditional long-standing assumptions about human motivation (which he labeled Theory X) in a 1957 article followed by a 1960 book titled *The Human Side of Enterprise.*[3] Theory X assumptions consist of the following:

- Employees are motivated primarily by economic incentives and will do whatever gives them the largest economic gain.
- Economic incentives are controlled by the organization, so employees should be regarded as passive agents, to be motivated and controlled by the organization.
- Feelings are irrational and must be prevented from interfering with employees' rational decisions of self-interest.
- Organizations must be designed in such a way as to neutralize and control employees' feelings.
- People are inherently lazy and therefore must be motivated by outside incentives.
- People must be controlled by external forces to ensure that they commit to organizational goals, since their personal goals will be in opposition to those of the organization.
- People are basically irrational and are incapable of self-discipline and control.
- People can be divided into two groups—those who fit the characteristics just outlined and those who are self-motivated and self-controlled; this latter group must assume responsibility for management.

The implications for management had been clear. Managers needed to make all decisions about what employees did and how they did it in an environment in which oversight and control were fundamental. The "psychological contract" between employees and the organization also was clear: economic rewards are given for work and obedience; the organization performs in such a way as to protect both itself and its employees from their irrational feelings through its control systems.

These assumptions were first shaken by the famous Hawthorne Studies in 1927, the most notable of which concerned the assembly of telephone relays.[4] Although the study has been justly criticized by later researchers for experimental design and control problems, its basic conclusions and its importance as a milestone in motivational research remain unshaken. In this study the researchers varied the illumination, rest periods, and refreshments of a selected study group. Each of these changes increased productivity. However, when the researchers took all of these changes away at the end of the study and returned the workers to their poorly lighted benches for long days of toil without rest, productivity increased even more, leading to the conclusion that the motivation to work, productivity, and the quality of the work produced might be influenced by factors other than simply work environment.

Further interviews indicated that it was primarily changes in the employees' attitude about their work that was producing the motivation to increase productivity. They were flattered by the attention being paid to them; interpersonal relationships among them, and between them and their supervisor, also had improved markedly. In short, psychological and social need gratification was increasing work productivity.

REVISIONISM: THEORY Y

Reflecting on this research and other studies that followed it, McGregor in 1957 suggested a contrasting set of assumptions about human nature that he described as Theory Y.[5] Its major tenets are:

- Most people can and will control their own work.
- Money is only one of the reasons people work.
- People's relationships with others are very important to them.
- Most employees enjoy at least some parts of their jobs.
- Employees seek to be mature on the job and will accept responsibility in a number of situations.

Maslow's work can add further insight into the nature of the "psychological contract" between employee and employer.[6] Maslow saw people as creatures of unending "wants" or needs—as soon as one was satisfied, another appeared to take its place. These needs are organized into a series of levels forming a hierarchy. At the lowest level are the physiological factors: food, water, shelter, etc. Next come safety needs, then the social needs for friendship, acceptance, and belonging. Esteem needs—a very important area for managerial thought and action, consist of two types: those that relate to the individual's reputation (respect, recognition, and status) and those involving self-esteem (self-confidence, independence, etc.). At the top of Maslow's "ladder" were self-fulfillment or self-actualization needs. This level, although he did not define it well, represents the combination of all of people's needs.

Maslow's contribution to the understanding of employee motivation stems primarily from the fact that before his work in 1943 it generally had been assumed that motivation was something that one person did to another. He demonstrated that a very significant portion of motivation came from having an internal need that drove the individual to take some kind of action. Since a satisfied need is never a motivator, management action should be directed toward unmet need at whatever level the employee has then reached. Although lower-level needs can be satisfied, those at the higher level almost never are.

THE TWO-FACTOR THEORY

In the 1950s Frederick Herzberg conducted a study of the importance of work and job conditions on the lives of average working people.[7] He concluded that the good feelings people had about their jobs were linked to job content, the bad feelings related mostly to job surroundings or what Herzberg called context. He called the good feelings motivators and the bad feelings hygiene factors. He felt that hygiene factors were prerequisites for effective motivation (i.e., job content) but were powerless to motivate by themselves.

Because his research identified two separate kinds of behaviors, one that satisfied and another that dissatisfied, it is called the Herzberg "Two-Factor Theory." This theory integrates well with Maslow's work in that the former's hygiene factors are similar to the latter's lower-level needs and Herzberg's motivators clearly relate to Maslow's belonging, esteem, and self-actualization needs.

These latter categories of needs are characterized by complexity, difficulty of satisfaction, and a need for continual support. Their ephemeral nature practically guarantees that such needs will never be satisfied. This review of the literature thus leads to the clear conclusion that managers will continue to deal many times with dissatisfied or unfulfilled employees. On the other hand, since satisfied needs do not motivate, it could well be argued that it is this plethora of unmet need and continual dissatisfaction that offers management's constant opportunities to initiate more effective motivation. Both authors' work demonstrates that the answer to more effective motivation lies in the concept of personal growth achieved through the work environment. Thus the target for management attention becomes how to best make the individuals' work more challenging and more meaningful.

Although it is indeed helpful and even necessary to understand the nature of the theories developed and their implications, it is the authors' perception that this does not provide a sufficient basis on which health care managers can ground their action in the future. Much of the research in the 1970s and early 1980s on this subject (available in a number of organizational psychology texts) demonstrated the extremely complex nature of management and motivation in particular.

The work of Hackman and his colleagues illustrates these points.[8] In the 1970s they developed a model containing a set of job factors that could be applied to any job. Their theory was that high levels of employee satisfaction (with concomitant high levels of motivation) and high performance for the organization would be achieved only if the employees could maintain three critical mental attitudes:

1. The work was perceived as inherently meaningful and worthwhile.
2. The work outcome was the direct product of the employees' efforts.
3. The employees were able to determine the results achieved in some regular and reliable way.

Hackman also identified three critical job dimensions: (1) the variety of the employee skills utilized, (2) the integrity of the task (in this context meaning the completeness or "wholeness" of the task or segment of work), and (3) the significance of the job (the extent to which it was perceived as substantial within the organization).

Levels of satisfaction also were influenced strongly by three additional factors—(1) whether the employees had the necessary skills to do the job, (2) the extent to which they had a need to grow and saw their work as growth producing, and (3) the extent to which they were satisfied with factors such as the social conditions, pay, and physical environment in the work setting. To the extent that managers decided a priori that job redesign could assist in motivating employees, this theory pointed out ways in which executives in a practical fashion could enrich work (by combining tasks, involving employees with clients, giving workers more of a voice in planning and controlling their work, etc.) to produce higher levels of organizational and employee satisfaction without really having to understand the reasons why the individuals were working in the first place.

COMPLEXITIES AND VARIABLES

Such studies demonstrate not only the almost overwhelming complexity of the individual employee but also the multiplicity of other variables that must be considered by managers setting out to provide leadership through better motivation. These include a realization that human needs can be expressed in almost endless variety, depending on individual life situations and stage of adult development, and that this hierarchy of need is variable not only from person to person but also from situation to situation and from time to time. Employees change as a result of their work experiences and may show different needs in different organizations or even different parts of the same organization. The nature of the work to be done, employees' individual abilities, and the organizational climate all may have significant influence on the effectiveness of work output and individual satisfaction. A study by Katz in 1978 indicated that the different job content factors studied by Hackman even varied in importance to the workers, depending on how long they had held their jobs.[9]

Examining all of this evidence from research, and reflecting on the many other situational variables specific to their own work environment, leaders might well throw up their hands in despair. How can they know where to begin to unravel such complex knots of fact, perception, need, and situation? A story concerning Mark Twain's early experience as a reporter is relevant. Twain had been instructed by his editor "never to state anything as a fact that he could not verify from personal knowledge." Sent to cover an important social event soon afterward, he turned in the following story:

> A woman giving the name of Mrs. James Jones, who is reported to be one of the social leaders of the city, is said to have given what purported to be a party yesterday to a number of alleged ladies. The hostess claims to be the wife of a reputed attorney.[10]

Are there really any rules of the road for practicing managers in this morass of complexity, "situationalism," and uncertainty or must they, like Twain, take refuge in ambiguity because of a lack of clear, hard fact?

FOUR LESSONS FOR MANAGERS

At least some lessons appear clear. The first is that health care managers clearly need to practice the same diagnostic discipline that their colleagues do in medicine but should direct their inquiry toward understanding and appreciating the differences in employees' skills, abilities, and motives.

Second, to the extent it is possible for each manager to do so, they all need to be flexible enough to behave differently toward subordinates out of the employees' need to be treated differently. This does not in any way contradict the evidence reported from research; rather, it is an affirmation of the fundamental fact that what may be highly effective in managers' behavior in motivating employees at some times in some situations will not work nearly as well at other times or with other employees.

Third, although it may not be regarded as particularly avant garde to do so, there are a number of situations and a significant number of employees who are quite comfortable with authority and will be managed (and motivated) most effectively by applying some or all of the Theory X principles. Neither theory is "good" or "bad" and therefore a rule to be followed at all times. The standard must be organizational effectiveness, not personal value judgments.

Fourth, a number of the "megatrends" identified by Naisbitt et al.— "decentralizing; reclaiming our traditional sense of self-reliance; demanding and getting a greater voice in government, business, and the marketplace; moving from hierarchies to networking, and demanding and getting a multitude of choices,"[11]—clearly point toward acceptance of the principles of Theory Y leadership as a dominant (but not exclusive) leadership style if the criterion is maximizing motivation. Once again it must be understood that motives and motivation are related to the values of the individuals, and each individual's values have been shaped and reinforced by a myriad of events and relationships within society.

In this examination of the importance of leadership style in building high levels of employee motivation, the authors state a clear initial bias: a participative, managed leadership style can assist individual managers in achieving improvement in motivation levels on an organizationwide basis. In a 1984 review of the research in this regard, Sashkin states: "The evidence of fifty years of action research clearly, consistently, and strongly demonstrates the effectiveness of participative management."[12] He reaffirms that this is a complex management approach, and favorably mentions research that concluded that the major difficulty with attempts to implement and maintain such programs is their tendency to have too much emphasis on "participative" and too little on "management." To this comment, the authors would add a resounding "Yes!" from their own experience.

Just as clearly, such a dominant organizational managerial style also fulfills certain basic human work and motivational needs. These were reviewed earlier in looking at Hackman's research; they were summarized by Sashkin as substantial control over managers' own behavior; completion of a whole, finished task; and satisfactory social or interpersonal contact within the work environment. Most managers in health care environments understand and have implemented such programs. They are mentioned here as a beginning point because they are fundamental to any organizationwide attempt to increase motivational levels.

CONTINGENCY THEORY

Above all, the challenge to managers is to be as intelligent and accepting as possible about recognizing differences and as flexible as possible in responding to them. Such flexibility and variable behavior have come to be called "contingency theory" in the literature in recognition of the fact that effective motivation is contingent upon a large number of situational variables.

However, although all this may form the basis for much of what individual managers will find satisfactory in relating to those directly around them, situational or contingency theory poses undeniable problems. By its very nature, it demands high levels of time, effective interpersonal communication, and experimentation. It is difficult for anyone who has long worked in an organizational environment to deny the reality of the perversity and complexity of human nature—it is seen all too frequently. But substantiation of its reality hardly serves as a complete (or even partial) basis for remedial action. Working managers' span of control, limits to the time they may devote to this particular pursuit, and the uncertainty of success and the speed of environmental change for the health care industry all argue strongly for other answers as well.

Also pertinent in this regard are managers' responsibilities as leaders: How can they move to bring about willingness for change, etc., in groups or teams of people to whom they relate episodically at best? The nature of the effort required to compensate for hospital occupancy rates that "slid from 75% in 1980 to 65% last year and may fall below 60% by 1990"[13] also argues for attention to motivation on an organizationwide basis.

In this context, it is important to address the issues of organizational climate, unifying system objectives and design, and the importance of a unifying organizational vision. This involves the perception that application of the principles reviewed earlier will assist managers in dealing directly with subordinates, peers, etc., but that in the present environment the standard for managerial motivation is higher than that.

Managers must come to see clearly that they must primarily rely on core organization values and culture as the predominant employee "control" system. Each of the organizations in which the authors work—Holy Names College and the Alta Bates Corporation—has a clearly defined and recognized culture that largely supplants the measurement, reward, and punishment control systems of more traditional organizations. The phrase "largely supplants" is used because those other control systems clearly continue to exist in each organization, but not as primary determinants of behavior for the majority of employees. Instead, the emphasis is on shared understandings of how each organization works and what its objectives, values, and traditions are. Such an emphasis has proved much more effective as a control system and much less expensive than its traditional counterparts.

SYSTEM DESIGN A MOTIVATOR

A further area for constructive change in producing organizationwide increases in motivation is that of unifying system design to encourage the desired behavior. The authors' experience indicates that not only the measurement (i.e., goal and objective accomplishment) system but also the selection and reward systems are important in this respect. Only since 1985 at Alta Bates Corporation, for instance, have there been consistent, structured initial attempts to include this value system's implications into hiring screening practices. It is possible, of course, to take a new employee who does not already accept or embrace the organization's value and cultural system and attempt to "socialize" him or her, but in the authors' experience this is a lengthy process with highly variable results. Why not try harder to find a motivational match on the front end? Health care managers have much to learn from the Walt Disney companies in this respect.[14] They carefully screen even the lowest-level employees, then orient them not only to specific job skills, but also to the history and values of the entire organization. Employees call each other by first names, and are expected to provide the best possible service for their "Guests"—paying guests, but never to be considered customers. The performance review process reflects this orientation toward excellence and service.

The authors have spent considerable time and effort redesigning managerial compensation programs in order to provide:

- increased attention toward short-term incentive programs based on attainment of work team goals
- the introduction of a long-term incentive program to attempt to provide some extended perspective to what has become a tendency to focus feverishly on short-term opportunity
- the introduction into the benefit program of many more choices and individual tailoring
- the introduction of broadly based employment continuity provisions for all executives.

The rapidity with which short-term strategies are changing and the need to pursue many different strategies for each individual business has led to closer examination of the potential benefits from more decentralized structures. The opportunity to increase motivational levels through placing decision-making authority closer to the lives of those directly affected was one important consideration.

This parallels a trend in many corporations to meld the processes of thinking and doing rather than maintaining the more traditional planning/deciding vs. implementing/operating schism. Some organizations have considered restructuring along product- or service-lines, giving managers greater responsibility for both planning and operations. Others, in making acquisitions of small companies, have offered those managers sabbaticals from operations and encouraged them to get into new program development. These efforts have been successful in that rank-and-file employees generate many useful program improvements and have a vested interest in championing their implementation, which is often vital to the survival of such efforts.

As a final suggestion of fruitful paths to effective employee motivation, managers should take the leader's role in establishing and maintaining corporate vision. In this sense, this is addressing the creation of a desired new state of affairs as well as the effective communication of that vision and efforts to keep it on track when obstacles arise. It has long been understood that managers are in control when their employees are exercising self-control. Buying into a shared vision creates such self-control, if that vision is conceived appropriately. That occurs when employees, as well as managers, see it as important for them personally and professionally. It must challenge employees in order to answer their desire to be committed to a purpose beyond their own personal needs. When effectively communicated, so that there is true buy-in by others, it becomes their vision as well. This is not to say that all individuals in the organization must share this vision, but when most do, it becomes an active funnel for drawing together a body of employees who want to move in a common direction. When this happens, the organization is said to have vision or purpose alignment.

OVERRIDING GOALS

Such vision alignment can produce significant changes in organizational performance since employees then will be doing what they need to do to move toward fulfilling their own personal objectives in life rather than "just working." The authors believe that appropriate overriding goals (in the sense of goals that can appeal to the deeply held values of a majority of employees) exist in the health care environment today. Executives and managers have an opportunity to bring into being systems that are integrated, effective, and efficient in delivering care to defined population bases in answer to a societal recognition that both the demand for and cost of health care was becoming too high. Such a vision of what the future could be has the ability to provide meaning and generate excitement for almost all persons at all levels. Management's task then becomes one of providing the enabling mechanisms and resource channeling necessary to convert vision into reality.

Yankelovich concludes that "though sparse, the survey data showing that Americans are growing less self-absorbed and better prepared to take a first step toward an ethic of commitment are fairly clear."[15] One site for such potential commitment is the workplace, and the health care organizations comprising part of it. It is sorely needed.

Can health care managers provide the leadership necessary to unleash such potential? If so, they must do so in the context of a recognition that a truly multivariate effort to awaken and then sustain the motivational levels necessary for such performance increases is what is required now.

NOTES

1. Ray Fitzgerald, *Boston Globe* (January 5, 1978), quoted in Edgar H. Schein, *Organizational Psychology* (Englewood Cliffs, N.J.: Prentice-Hall, Inc., 1980).

2. Daniel Yankelovich, "New Rules in American Life: Searching for Self-Fulfillment in a World Turned Upside Down," *Psychology Today* (April 1981):76.

3. Douglas McGregor, *The Human Side of Enterprise* (New York: McGraw-Hill, 1960).

4. E. Mayo, *The Human Problems of an Industrial Civilization* (Cambridge, Mass.: Harvard University Press, 1933) and F.J. Roethlisberger and W. Dickson, *Management and the Worker* (Cambridge, Mass.: Harvard University Press, 1939).

5. McGregor, *Human Side.*

6. Abraham H. Maslow, "A Theory of Human Motivation," *Psychological Review* 80 (1943):370–396.

7. Frederick Herzberg, B. Mausner, and B. Snyderman, *The Motivation to Work* (New York: John Wiley & Sons, Inc., 1959).

8. J.R. Hackman and E.E. Lawler, "Employee Reactions to Job Characteristics," *Journal of Applied Psychology Monograph* (1971):259–286. J.R. Hackman and G.R. Oldham, *Work Redesign* (Reading, Mass: Addison-Wesley, 1979).

9. R. Katz, "Job Longevity as a Situational Factor in Job Satisfaction," *Administrative Science Quarterly* 23 (1978):204–223.

10. Jacob M. Braude, "Human Interest Stories," *Complete Speaker's and Toastmaster's Library* (Englewood Cliffs, N.J.: Prentice-Hall, Inc., 1965).

11. Tom Richman, "Peering Into Tomorrow," *Inc.* (October 1982):47–48.

12. Marshall Sashkin, "Participative Management Is an Ethical Imperative," *Organizational Dynamics* (Spring 1984):7.

13. "Don't Expect Any Miracles at the Hospitals," *Business Week* (January 13, 1986):98.

14. N.W. Pope, "Mickey Mouse Marketing," *American Banker* (July 25, 1979). "More Mickey Mouse Marketing," *American Banker* (September 12, 1979), as quoted in T.S. Peters and R.H. Waterman, Jr., *In Search of Excellence* (New York: Harper & Row, Publishers, Inc., 1982):167–168. Interview with former Disneyland employee.

15. Yankelovich, "New Rules," 89.

BIBLIOGRAPHY

Berlew, David E. "Leadership and Organizational Excitement." *California Management Review* 17, no. 2 (Winter 1974):21–30.

Blake, Robert R., and Jane Srygley Mouton. "A Comparative Analysis of Situationalism and 9,9 Management by Principle." *Organizational Dynamics* (Spring 1982):20–42.

Chusmir, Leonard H. "How Fulfilling Are Health Care Jobs?" *Health Care Management Review* 11, no. 1 (Winter 1986):27–32.

Cummings, Larry L. "Compensation, Culture and Motivation: A Systems Perspective." *Organizational Dynamics* (Winter 1984):33–44

Harman, Willis W. "Visions of Tomorrow: The Transformation Ahead." *OD Practitioner* 13, no. 1 (February 1981):1–10.

Health Central Corporation. *Environmental Assessment, Moving Forward: An Integration of Interests,* 1985.

Herzberg, Frederick. *Work and the Nature of Man* (Cleveland, Ohio: World Publishing Company, 1966).

―――. "One More Time: How Do You Motivate Employees?" In *How Successful Executives Handle People, 12 Studies on Communications and Management Skills.* Cambridge, Mass.: Harvard Business Review, 1970, 82–91.

Kaplan, Robert E. "Trade Routes: The Manager's Network of Relationships." *Organizational Dynamics* (Spring 1984):37–52.

Kiefer, Charles F., and Peter M. Senge. *Metanoic Organizations: Experiments in Organizational Innovation.* Innovation Associates Inc., 1982.

Kipnis, David, Stuart Schmidt, Chris Swaffin-Smith, and Ian Wilkinson. "Patterns of Managerial Influence: Shotgun Managers, Tacticians, and Bystanders." *Organizational Dynamics* (Winter 1984).

Lassey, William R., and Marshall Sashkin, eds. *Leadership and Social Change,* 3rd ed. San Diego: University Associates, 1983.

New England Hospital Assembly Inc. *Motivational Dynamics, Mainsprings of Motivation,* Unit I. Minneapolis: Control Data Corporation, 1975.

Peters, Thomas J. "Putting Excellence into Management." *Business Week* (July 21, 1980):196–205.

Pinchott, Gifford, III. *Intrapreneuring.* New York: Harper & Row, Publishers, Inc., 1985.

Richman, Tom. "Peering Into Tomorrow," *Inc.* (October 1982):47–48.

Sashkin, Marshall. "Participative Management Is an Ethical Imperative." *Organizational Dynamics* (Spring 1984):5–21.

Schein, Edgar H. *Organizational Psychology.* 3rd ed., edited by Richard S. Lazarus, Englewood Cliffs, N.J. Prentice-Hall, Inc., 1980.

————. *Organizational Culture and Leadership.* San Francisco: Jossey-Bass, Inc., Publishers, 1985.

Wilson, John W., and Vicky Cahan. "Don't Expect Any Miracles at the Hospitals." *Business Week* (January 13, 1986):98.

Yankelovich, Daniel. "New Rules in American Life: Searching for Self-Fulfillment in a World Turned Upside Down." *Psychology Today* (April 1981):35–91.

Effective Communications

Dan S. Wilford

5

For successful managers, effective communications are not just important, they are a make-or-break accountability factor. There is a direct relationship between the ability to manage and the ability to communicate; effective management cannot be achieved without effective communications. The purpose, values, strategic plans, goals, programs, services, projects, and priorities of the organization are of little significance if they are not well executed through a comprehensive communications program.

The complexity of the health care industry dictates that effective communications must be high on the priority list of all executives. Outstanding communications skills are vital in managing the hospital conglomerate. Today's hospital executive must deal effectively with 20 to 30 "businesses" within the same organization, converse with a lay governing board, a medical staff with its own jargon, diverse employee groups, and a public that has little comprehension of the complexities of the facility's community. Each group demands and deserves to know what is going on in the organization. Each group represents a different facet of hospital operations; it is management's challenge to develop a consistency of understanding within and among these groups. In this myriad of complex activity and audiences, hospital managers cannot be effective if they cannot communicate well with every segment of their organization and their public.

A great deal of material has been written on effective communications. Health care managers would be wise to include them in their personal continuing education programs. This chapter outlines some basic principles of communications that are applicable to hospital executives. It also discusses specific techniques that can be used in communicating with the governing board, medical staff, management staff, employees, and the public.

PRINCIPLES OF EFFECTIVE COMMUNICATIONS

The key to effective communication is remembering the basics. Communications reflect a value system; therefore, when communicating, executives must never violate their conscience. Managers' own intuitive feelings and value systems dictate that communications be honest. Total honesty eliminates the need for concern about getting involved in a compromising or conflicting situation. To make errors in communications is human—it also is inevitable. But dishonesty in communications is unforgivable.

When communicating, executives must be realistic about their talents and abilities. Some managers have a more natural talent for communicating than others, and some have learned communications skills better than others. To communicate effectively, they must recognize their strengths and weaknesses and develop resources to improve their overall approach. Communications consultants, advertising agencies, marketing experts, and other related professionals may be useful in developing these skills. However, it is important for every manager to have an authentic communications style in order to maintain credibility. Maximizing strengths and compensating for weaknesses are important as managers develop their communications strategies.

Openness is another principle of management communications. More than ever, governing boards, medical staffs, management teams, employees, and, certainly, the public, expect openness in communications. Managers must protect confidential information, but in general it is expected that they be open about hospital activities. For an organization to have open communications with the public, it is important to have established guidelines, policies, and procedures authorizing appropriate individuals to be spokespersons. If a knowledgeable person is authorized to speak for the organization, openness seldom can put the institution in jeopardy. Without complete knowledge, however, openness is high-risk communications.

A positive attitude must be shown in all communication efforts. In the hospital industry, there are negative situations, issues, concerns, and activities; however, a positive approach results in upbeat communications. Organizations and the public are bogged down with negative communications so, to be effective, managers must demonstrate a positive attitude in their communication practices.

Another major principle in effective communications is sincerity. Credibility can be achieved only through sincerity; without it, silence should be the policy.

Communications must be within the range of perception of the recipients. Managers communicate effectively by using different phrases, terms, and styles, depending upon their particular audiences. Regardless of the audience, simplicity helps in communicating clear, concise, understandable messages.

Timing also is a major factor in determining communications' effectiveness. A good decision at the wrong time is a bad decision. In paraphrase, it might also be said that good communications presented at the wrong time is poor communications. Properly timed, communications may be used to inspire and motivate people; the same information presented at the wrong time may be totally ineffective.

These basic principles are applicable regardless of the group with which managers are communicating. In the following sections, ideas and techniques that can be helpful in communicating with the governing board, medical staff, management staff, employees, and the public are presented. The principles of communications should be applied to all of these groups.

COMMUNICATIONS WITH THE GOVERNING BOARD

The hospital executive has a unique and nondelegable obligation to establish strong communications with the governing board, which is legally and morally responsible for all of the organization's activities. Since most hospital governing boards serve on a voluntary basis, the very least that management can do is to keep them totally informed on matters of interest and concern. Unless the members have unusual longevity and experience, they are governing an organization that, in many respects, is foreign to them.

Because of the tremendous volume of information that needs to be conveyed to the board members about hospital activities, it is critical that the executive develop a disciplined system of providing routine communications to them. Without a mechanism to feed such information continually, long and intense board and committee meetings would be necessary just to keep the members abreast of significant issues. The board deserves to receive information in a continuing flow so that it has a base of knowledge regarding the hospital's operations; the dissemination of such information should not be limited to the panel's meetings.

A Weekly Activity Report is an excellent mechanism to provide the board with continuous information. This report is best written by the chief executive officer at the end of the week, informing the board of major activities that took place during the week. This type of report has the advantage of giving the members a reasonable amount of information that can be digested on a weekly basis. It provides members with early notice of major issues, problems, and concerns that they will be dealing with—probably at a formal meeting. This report provides the CEO with a complete, historical record documenting the institution's major activities. It also serves as a referral document in routine management activities. By sharing the board's weekly activity report with senior management staff members, the CEO keeps them abreast of the facility's overall activities, some of which they are not exposed to on a week-to-week basis.

The Weekly Activity Report may be styled much like a *Kiplinger Letter.* It is presented in layman's terms and in informal style. It usually contains two to four pages. Its preparation requires considerable effort by the CEO but, as discussed later, it can be used as a basic document in communicating with other groups. If the organization has a large governing board and effectively utilizes an executive committee for most operational decision making, the report may be directed to that body. In such cases, a Monthly Activity Report (a composite of the Weekly Activity Reports) can be sent to the full board on a monthly basis. The decision as to which approach to use depends upon the board's desire for information.

Responsible communication with the board also includes directing issues to the appropriate committees. Just as the Marines need a "few good men," hospital organizations need "a few good committees." Assuming that the committee structure is streamlined and efficient, it is important to provide selective communications to the committees. Proper directing of information to the individual committees can help their members focus on their particular roles and the specific concerns for which they have responsibility.

The minutes of board and committee meetings provide excellent feedback to board members. Minutes should be mailed to the various members one week after the meeting. This lets those who were absent to be brought up to date on a timely basis and those who were present to suggest any corrections or additions, again on a timely basis. In addition to the minutes, the secretary can prepare a one-page Summary of Action Report. This succinctly states the actions taken by the committee. It can be mailed to board members individually, weekly with the Weekly Activity Report, or held for meetings to give them a quick summary of all committees' activities.

Another vehicle for maintaining effective communications with the board is to place the members on the mailing list for all hospital public relations materials. Mailing articles and other information that address particular concerns or issues of the hospital organization also is advised.

On many occasions, the executive needs to communicate with board members on matters in which written materials and/or telephone calls are not adequate or appropriate. It is important to have an established rapport so that the executive can deal with numerous issues on a personal, eyeball-to-eyeball basis. Nothing takes the place of personal communications in perceiving the feelings of board members on various issues. The members' feelings as expressed in reacting to such communications often are more significant than the presentation of the information.

In dealing with governing boards it is a cardinal sin to surprise them—except where extraordinarily confidential issues are discussed. The CEO should never present a major issue or concern for the first time at a board meeting. Although they are accustomed to dealing with major policy issues, few board members are prepared to cope with them on a crisis basis. By adhering to the techniques presented in this section, executives should be able to avoid surprising the board.

COMMUNICATIONS WITH THE MEDICAL STAFF

The style and nature of the hospital executive's communications with the medical staff depend upon many factors, including the medical staff's size, diversity, loyalty, and knowledge. The nature of the issue being discussed also determines the appropriate manner of communication. The principles that apply to other communications certainly are valid for dealing with the medical staff. There also are other important considerations in communicating with physicians:

- The executive, presenting new ideas to physicians, should be prepared to offer the new concept or idea three times. Often, the response to the first presentation is negative. The second presentation creates some understanding of the issue or concept. After the third presentation, if it is a good idea, the executive can expect acceptance. Patience is virtue in communicating with doctors.
- The executive should establish rapport with physicians on their turf. They will feel more comfortable if the executive walks the deck in the hospital and talks with them on the nursing units and in the clinical areas. To gain acceptance and develop open relationships with physicians, the executive needs to communicate with them informally in their own environment, including their offices.
- The executive must respect the formal organization of the medical staff but it also is necessary to approach the informal leadership in order to establish effective communications. Certain doctors on every medical staff can spread the word, or disseminate the information, effectively. Others purposely should be avoided when communicating informally.
- The executive in communicating about controversial issues, must avoid putting any physician on the spot. Differences of opinion are best resolved in small groups or on an individual basis, not in a group setting where there is high risk of embarrassment.
- The executive can use the patient as a common denominator in communications about controversial issues or when discussing services and

programs. If the CEO and doctor both focus on what is best for the patient, then insignificant issues can be avoided and meaningful communications maintained.

The medical staff members deserve to know what is going on in the institution and about actions taken by the governing board that can affect their practice. They deserve to know where the hospital resources are being utilized. They need to be aware of all patient programs and services. They should have input regarding the management of the hospital and the governing board. Members of the medical staff should serve on the governing board and on its committees, elected under the same criteria as nonmedical members and for the same reason—a genuine interest in the organization and in the health and well-being of the community. They should be expected to represent the community on the board and not to serve the vested interest of the medical staff or themselves. Their involvement at this level of the organization provides valuable clinical input into policymaking and fosters a trust relationship among the governing board, management, and medical staff. Effective communications with medical staff demands physician involvement.

The medical staff members deserve to receive routine communications from management. The Weekly Activity Report is a good source of material from which to develop a Monthly Activity Report for physicians. They, too, should receive all hospital public relations materials, which should include news and features about them.

Management must participate in the regular meetings of the medical staff, clinical departments, and all medical staff committees. This day-to-day involvement fosters close relationships, credibility, and timely decisionmaking that is so important in developing effective communications.

Communications can be enhanced by having nonagenda meetings with physicians. The idea is to have small groups convene for lunch (or breakfast) and simply ask the question, "If you were chief executive officer of this organization, what changes would you make?" Being an objective listener to the responses is essential for the CEO.

COMMUNICATIONS WITH MANAGEMENT STAFF AND EMPLOYEES

In addition to the governing board and medical staff, a third part of the hospital family with whom effective communications must be maintained is the employees. Fran Tarkenton, one-time all-pro quarterback in the National Football League and currently a management consultant, presents one of the simplest and most accurate prescriptions for motivating people:

(1) Management must set the example for employees. (2) Management must communicate to employees the organization's plans and goals—where the institution is going. (3) Management must give employees feedback on organizational accomplishments.' The result of all this should be good personnel relations and motivated employees.

Some techniques that can be used with the management staff to ensure effective communications include the following:

- Periodic management staff meetings will enable all members reporting to the chief executive officer to hear the same thing at the same time. Depending on the size and nature of the organization, these meetings may be held weekly, biweekly, or monthly. To ensure maximum attendance, they should be established for a specific regular time.
- One-on-one sessions should be held with all management personnel with whom a manager works directly. This permits direct, confidential communications about operational matters. These sessions should be held weekly or biweekly.
- Communications are greatly enhanced by an open-door policy. Most responsible managers will not abuse this privilege. Timely, responsive, quality communications can result from properly utilizing this approach.
- Short management retreats can be effective, particularly when discussions are focused on the organization's strategic plans, goals, and objectives. Management team building is a result of such communications. Quarterly retreats of a day and a half to two days are recommended. They need not be expensive. The best results normally come from meeting outside of the immediate work environment, but out-of-town trips and resorts are not required. Occasionally, it is healthy to get away from the office and involve staff members' spouses in some of the activities. These relationships can enhance communications, understanding, and trust.

Effective managers have effective communications with the troops. However, vertical communication is not totally effective because of roadblocks in the organizational line. It is important for the employees periodically to see the top management staff, particularly the chief executive officer, and to have the opportunity to communicate directly. Techniques that have been proved successful in many well-run organizations include the following:

- Walking the deck is an effective way to communicate with employees in the trenches. The purpose of these informal visits is not to solve all of the employees' problems but to give them a feel for the organization and to develop a rapport with them—they need to know that senior management is interested in them.

- Managers should have quarterly, informal rap sessions with employees on all shifts. These need not be mandatory unless managers need to communicate critical information to everyone. Such sessions can update employees on the institution's major activities and also provide opportunities so they can ask questions directly of managers.

- All employees deserve to attend a monthly departmental meeting with the executive who has responsibility for their work. This forces the department head to be visible and accessible to employees on all shifts, at least once a month. It also enables the executive to communicate organizational activities as well as departmental goals, priorities, and progress on a regular basis.

- Management should promote a process through which employees can make suggestions for improvements, new programs, and services. Some hospitals have found the quality circles concept to be effective. Quality circles is a management concept developed in Japan wherein small groups meet to identify and resolve problems at the workplace. A presentation is made to top management identifying the problems and recommending solutions. It is a grass-roots approach to problem solving and participatory management. Other organizations have established futures groups among employees to generate and encourage new ideas. Futures groups are groups appointed by top management to concentrate on what will happen in the future and how the organization must prepare to deal with future changes. They are not allowed to concentrate on today's issues, but rather to totally concentrate on the future. Involving employees throughout the organization in annual goal setting and evaluation is another way to ensure participation. Each institution should develop mechanisms to encourage innovative and creative communications.

- Hospital managers occasionally should send letters to employees at their homes. These might be a year-end letter of appreciation for their hard work, a greeting to their family during a religious holiday season, a birthday greeting, an annual progress report on the condition of the organization, or other such matters. This is a good way of communicating specific messages to employees but, perhaps even more important, it is a technique through which employees' spouses and other family members can receive information that helps them identify with the organization. All improvements in wages and salaries and in benefits program should be communicated to employees at their homes so family members will be aware of the organization's concern.

- Employees are an organization's best source of advertising and as such must be included in the distribution of employee newsletters, magazines, and other public relations materials regarding programs and services.

A unique communications program has been implemented by Memorial Care Systems in Houston. To communicate with employees in seven hospitals and in several other work locations away from the corporate headquarters, a monthly videocassette is produced and distributed throughout the system. This 15- to 30-minute "video newsletter" is shown at departmental meetings each month. Addressed to employees and covering major events throughout the system, it is available for viewing on all shifts. An interview with the corporate president is included and he responds to a hot line that has received calls from employees during the preceding month. This has been so popular that many medical staff members watch it regularly. It also is shown on the in-house closed-circuit television system that can be viewed in patient rooms. Patients are impressed that employees are being informed about corporate activity. It also promotes good patient relations.

The best marketing resource for a hospital is its employees. They can have a dramatic impact on patients utilizing hospital services. They also can be spokespersons for the hospital out in the community. Effective communications with employees is vital to the success of a health care organization.

COMMUNICATING WITH THE PUBLIC

In communicating with the public, it is important to maintain all principles of communications that are used with other groups. It is important to realize also that the public's view of the health industry is more cynical than at any other time in history. Costs are high and, in times of economic distress, health care providers and organizations are facing unusual scrutiny and pressures. Of even greater concern is the increasing public distrust of such American institutions that seldom were criticized in the past. Educational institutions, health care facilities, churches, the medical profession, the legal profession, even the judiciary system—all of these have lost credibility with the public. This must be realized by executives in the health care industry.

There are many techniques that can be used to communicate with the public. Hospitals continue to use annual reports, magazines or journals, monthly newsletters, news releases, human interest stories, and, more recently, advertising in the various media (radio, television, newspaper, direct mail, etc.). All of these techniques should be considered and used, based on the institution's particular situation.

For years executives in the health industry concentrated on how to communicate to the public; now, they must focus their attention on how to communicate with the public.

Memorial Care Systems in Houston uses another innovative new approach to communicate openly and genuinely with the public regarding its purpose, values, strategic plans, goals, and performance. Memorial has developed a computer-assisted communication system that uses a computer and computer pads (simple input terminals) to gather opinions from local groups of up to 200. Groups representing the hospital's constituencies— volunteers, business leaders, political leaders, professional men and women—are asked to meet and provide input. After introductory comments and directions, a battery of questions and/or statements are given to the group, and the members respond by inputting a number on the computer pad corresponding with their attitude.

For example, a statement might be, "The cost of care is my major concern in selecting a health facility." Participants would enter #1 if they agree strongly, #2 if they agree, #3 if they are neutral, #4 if they disagree, and #5 if they disagree strongly. The results then are computed and projected on a large screen in front of the group, allowing immediate feedback.

Consensus data constitute a worthwhile form of communication for the organization as to participants' feelings, attitudes, values, and priorities. The screen projections are used to stimulate discussion. Invariably, the data stimulate in-depth discussion of why people feel as they do. Memorial representatives can deal with issues and concerns at that time, or they can take the data, study them, and communicate with the group later as to the company's response to (and use of) this input.

Those are examples of the kinds of creative efforts that the health care industry must develop in order to communicate with the public in a meaningful way. Members of the public need to feel that they have had meaningful input into shaping the future of the changing health care industry.

Effective communication is critical in today's society and will grow in importance. Effective executives in the health care industry should be keenly aware of some of the basic principles of communication that have been presented here.

Communications is the most dynamic of all human processes. Effective managers will continue the search for techniques in communicating with the groups that are vital to the success of their organization.

The Management of Stress

Robert L. Wall

6

"Take one of these Valium every six hours and . . ." If this oft-repeated medical prescription sounds familiar, it probably is because it is one of the most widely utilized treatment alternatives for dealing with stress, the most common threat to modern society's physical and mental health. Publications from medical journals to supermarket magazines bombard their readers with purported remedies or behavior modifications to relieve people's lives of the manifestations of stress in their daily living activities.

Coping with stress is an inseparable part of the decision-making process that every manager faces. Health care managers, in particular, need to understand stress, its sources, implications, and consequences, then deal with it in an informed manner in order to stay healthy and productive. Such managers have to deal not only with the usual business demands of the enterprise but also with the extra and unique health care aspects, which sometimes are in conflict with business decisions. Health care managers unable to distinguish these conflicting forces are good candidates for eventual burnout.

UNDERSTANDING STRESS

Stress is defined as the body's response to the external and internal stimuli that prepare it to deal with a particular stressor. Stress progresses through three increasingly severe stages or levels.

The first is an alarm reaction that prepares the body for a fight-or-flight response. In this stage, the respiration rate increases, the heart beats faster, the adrenalin level rises, and people unconsciously prepare their primitive survival skills for use. Health care managers, particularly those in a hospital setting, may recognize this first stage as the response to a doctor furious

71

about an emergency room call schedule or a delay in getting lab or X-ray reports. Although acute at the time, this first stage stress usually is brief and passes rapidly.

The second level results from the body's inability to repair itself from the results of first-level stress. When stress continues without relief, the body's adaptation mechanism starts to fail. Indicators such as gastrointestinal symptoms, urinary tract difficulties, or cardiorespiratory irregularities become evident. Stress manifestations at the second level begin to affect severely the managers' decision-making ability because of the need to deal with the illnesses that have begun.

The third level of stress brings exhaustion, inability to concentrate, insomnia, and other complications, and the body and mind no longer can cope. The consequence of stress is manifested now by emotional disturbance and a variety of physical illnesses affecting any or all bodily systems. Most individuals can identify this stage and its effect on themselves or their friends and associates.

Despite the obvious deleterious effects of stress, it has certain beneficial attributes that managers can use if they can identify and control them. In a stress condition at the initial level, people actually think better and react faster, so some stress is desirable. The question is whether they can control and manage stress or will fall prey to its pressures. Therefore, managers need to know more about this good news-bad news situation and how they can take advantage of its benefits while avoiding its dangers.

HOW STRESS LEVELS ARE REACHED

As Alvin Toffler explains in his books *Future Shock* and *The Third Wave,* the intensity and frequency of change in the modern era have created stress levels of great magnitude. Society runs the risk of being unable to develop adaptive mechanisms to deal with wave after wave of change. In their lifetimes, managers have seen the change cycle move from infrequent to rapid. Basic reference points of human existence that once seemed unchangeable are being challenged and changed with increasing rapidity. Traditional family units and relationships, religious doctrine and practice, economic relationships, political structures, education, and health care are a few elements of the human environment that have undergone change that amounts to complete societal revolution. In the space of a single lifetime of threescore years and ten, persons have seen extraordinary technological and scientific discoveries, now accepted as commonplace, that have permitted the human species to multiply and occupy virtually any space on earth and to explore the firmament, significantly:

- safe drinking water
- sanitary sewage systems
- uncontaminated food supply, readily available
- widespread availability of electricity, which has changed mankind from daytime only to a 24-hour species
- medical advances and a lengthened life span of relative comfort
- transportation advances, including space travel
- nuclear energy, with its direct and indirect impact on the population base, depending on the political decisions made regarding its use
- communications, including much wider literacy, telephone, radio, TV, satellites, the computerization of society, and instantaneous information transfer.

These developments illustrate humans' need for an internal mechanism that will allow them to acclimate to ever-changing circumstances. The author marvels at the change that has occurred in the lifetime of his parents and at their capacity not only to absorb and accept the transformations they have witnessed but also to adapt so well as to use the changes for their benefit.

In this writer's view, the greatest impact of all the great changes of the last hundred years has been on society's basic unit, the family. A family unit, once nearly self-sufficient and independent, now must interact with every other unit in society to obtain the basic necessities of life. The single fact of such remarkable interdependence causes enormous personal stress. Most of the world's population is centered on urban centers. Housing, food, water, utilities, sewage disposal, and earning capacity have shifted people away from a self-sufficient life style that was millions of years in the making.

Therefore, individuals are stressed both at home and in the workplace by factors that can have a powerful cumulative effect.

STRESS PROBLEMS OF HEALTH CARE MANAGERS

In addition to the expected societal and family stresses, health care managers face added layers of stress because of the peculiar occupational idiosyncrasies of their industry and its delivery system. Such stress factors include:

- The urgency of life-and-death decisions laid onto the hospital and other delivery points that transform most decisions from those such as in ordinary business into ethical and highly charged emotional issues as well.

- The delicate relationships that exist among the groups forming the power base of health care institutions. Medical staff, specialized health workers, trustees, and administrators prove to be particularly difficult to deal with. Each special interest group is seeking constantly to expand its sphere of influence and power based on its own agenda. Mediating among these groups demands the application of unusual skills by health care managers in the decision-making process, which creates its own unique form of stress.

- The complex organization in a health care institution that provides managers with their greatest difficulty—trying to get dissimilar groups to work together toward the facility's goals. The most familiar institution in health care is the hospital. Managing a hospital is different from managing the usual corporation.

- The governing board (in addition to all the diverse groups that work inside or around the hospital), which also can be viewed as a narrow specialty group. It is as difficult to get its members to pull in the same direction as it is with other specialty employee groups or doctors. Managers who are unsuccessful in leading the governing group, whether it is called the trustees, directors, or board, toward a common goal, will find their stress level will increase. Executives unable to coalesce the governing body, medical staff, specialty employees, and administration in today's fast-changing health care environment rapidly become ineffective, causing the institution to suffer and everyone's stress level to rise.

- The level of outside regulatory influence and its great impact that can leave health care managers with higher stress levels because of its effect on the decision-making process. Federal, state, and local laws (regulations from civil rights, to diagnosis related group [DRG] payment, to local zoning laws) have multiplied exponentially, and no end is in sight. Added to all these restrictions are accreditation standards for all the various groups trying to impose their own constraints. Constant changes by outside regulatory groups complicate the decision-making process—and decision making is the raison d'être of managers. Inability to make decisions quickly and effectively erodes executives' leadership ability, creates high frustration levels, and raises the cost of the services they are responsible for providing.

- The threat of malpractice suits from patients not accepting the limitations of medical treatment. Public expectation is conditioned to expect answers to all questions and solutions for all problems. In a hospital or other health care facility, the product is called "care." These institutions are expected to deliver care that provides daily miracles, with 100 percent success, and at an economical rate. Health care executives realize the public expectation of perfection is unattainable, which adds another layer of frustration, a perceived sense of incompetence, a lower self-image, and resultant stress.

The scenario of today's rapid-fire changes, greater demands for current knowledge, state-of-the-art technology, new systems, new markets, reorganization needs, new payment strategies, new rights issues, government regulation, etc., set the stage for stressed health care executives who are so overwhelmed with the job that many find it impossible to cope. As a result, they have four choices:

- leave and move to new location with less stress
- leave and change to career with different or less stress
- stay and face resulting possible loss of emotional and/or physical health
- stay and face possible "burnout."

Burnout can have a devastating effect not only on careers of health care executives but also on the institutions they represent. Enthusiasm and effectiveness are lost or become stagnant. There is a tremendous domino effect that may affect all levels of the organization. Burned out executives do not have the initiative to pursue higher career goals, motivate employees, promote company growth, or effectively manage companies' day-to-day activities.

The question to ask, then, is: If being a health care executive is so stressful, why is anyone in the field? The answer is obvious: There are effective ways to adapt and cope, and the goal of improving health care is compelling. No doubt, the complexities inherent in health care will continue and intensify, particularly in the new dichotomous era of cost containment versus quality care.

With those circumstances as their prospect, how do executives develop the skills of managing the institutions and managing stress? Ways must be found to control both processes if health care management is to continue to be a desirable career objective.

The author's formula for avoiding the Valium route is a nonmedical, three-dose prescription for health care executives that seems to help them in coping. They should:

1. Identify stress factors and their source: at work, within the family, and in social relationships. Instead of spending time worrying, they should analyze and identify specific stressors.

2. Start modifying the impact of these stress factors by educating themselves and those they deal with, then choose their fight-or-flight strategy.
3. Manage their own person as a resource with the same accountability as they manage the institution or job. As noted, stress cannot be eliminated, but managers can learn how to control their lives to deal with it.

IDENTIFYING STRESS FACTORS AND SOURCES

In stress management, as in war, targeting the enemy is an essential first step. The key question is: Where is the stress coming from? Even when it appears to be coming from all sides, executives should pinpoint specific factors that seem heaviest, most threatening, or imminent. It is easier for executives to plot strategy for dealing with definite issues or specific relationships than to feel they are battling a nebulous-gray-everything-everybody. For example:

If executives have a serious problem at home with

- a troubled or handicapped child
- an elderly parent requiring new housing and care arrangements
- a decisive rift with mate or a romantic relationship

the resulting very real and heavy feelings are difficult to put aside when they enter the office to face the institution's day-to-day problems. Conversely, it is difficult to leave problems at the office, and managers carry over work stress that affects their personal relationships with loved ones or friends. Sometimes just sorting and listing helps lighten the load by making the stress source visible and distinct from the areas in which executives are having more success or feel more sense of control and competency. This distinction helps them keep a sense of balance.

Again, as on the battlefield, distinguishing foe from friend can be confusing. In the pressure of the workplace, any new stress factor may appear to be an enemy at first. It is helpful in identifying stressors to remember the beneficial attributes that can confuse foe and friend. Factors that begin as stress can:

1. force a change that brings long-range improvement; without this prodding, the situation would have been left at status quo and would have proved to be a larger problem later

2. become a stimulant to creativity, a challenge for improved strategy or organization.

By accepting an attitude of challenge, it sometimes is possible to change foe to friend.

MODIFYING STRESS IMPACT

As soon as the most critical stress factors have been identified, executives can plan their strategy for flight or fight to control or modify the impact of each specific problem. To map their plan, they first must be armed with all the information about the stressor they can get. It is time to use the best resources and to be thorough and unrelenting until they know the facts. If the stressor is work related, the managers' resources might include:

- pertinent publications
- national and state journals
- special legislative bulletins
- specialized professional consultation
- relevant health care associations, their library, or their personnel.

Thus equipped, executives may find alternative tactics surfacing.

For purposes here, "flight" strategy can be defined as retreating or falling back for regrouping, and ignoring or avoiding confrontation. Some problems can be handled by evasive maneuvers to stall for a time advantage.

If "fight" is the chosen response, managers already have begun preparation by educating themselves. Next, they choose who their assistants will be and educate all those with whom they deal on this issue. Nothing beats good preparation, and it is essential to educate those who will be involved about what is likely to come. Medical staff, trustees, department heads, and all employees respond positively when they know what is happening that might affect them. This advice works equally well in work or social relationships.

Now, executives are equipped to search for solutions or alternatives. They have some armor, and the stressor is becoming more like a challenge than just a threat. They are fully alert to the possible strengths and weaknesses of their position and can attend to further preparation.

It is possible to counter or alter the problem by direct involvement with it, e.g., by participation in the legislative process through group influence or by other collective action. By taking an active role in specialty organizations and health associations at local, state, and national levels, health care executives can educate legislators to their needs and concerns. This route for effecting change in legislation can help reduce the severity of stress by affording a measure of control and input into laws that affect work. Fortunately, through education to help plot out strategy in dealing with tough issues, preparation for those to be affected by the issues' outcome, and participation in a support group for added information and collective clout, executives can reduce the impact of workplace stress appreciably. The same tools could be adapted to many personal problems.

Whether the problem (stressor) is work related or home related, magic solutions should not be expected to erase all worry, pain, or burden. This discussion describes only tools for reducing the impact of stress, modifying frustration, and, it is to be hoped, providing a coping framework.

MANAGING THE MANAGER

This final dose of the prescription—executives' managing themselves—occasionally may be the only viable tool or method for dealing with stressful situations. Nearly always it is the most significant factor in determining the degree of success in coping. What is involved in managing one's person as a resource with the same accountability as managing an institution?

Executives are diligent in guarding obvious resources such as investments, buildings, transportation vehicles, etc., to see that they stay in balance or in tip-top condition. They must take at least as much care of themselves to keep in healthy balance—physically, mentally, emotionally, spiritually. This is such an obvious factor that managers tend to ignore it until ulcer, heart attack, stroke, or depression rearrange their priorities and force them into new patterns of living with better balance.

This last dose of the prescription for coping now becomes the theme for the rest of this chapter because it is the most critical variable. All the identifying, education, and strategy preparation will be of little value if managers fail to manage themselves and become severely out of balance.

BALANCING EXECUTIVES' LIVES

Executives cannot afford the luxury of allowing themselves to get out of balance in their lives. There must be equal parts of what may be called a living formula:

- family or close friends, food, and home
- work and work-related activities

- spiritual matters
- recreation
- rest and relaxation.

Imbalance in any of these areas puts executives into an unbalanced framework and makes them high-risk stress candidates.

Physical and mental health need good preventive care. Most people do not think twice about the money or effort it takes to perform routine maintenance on their automobiles. As a matter of fact, some individuals are much more thoughtful and caring about their mechanical conveyances than of themselves, spouse, and family. There should be a way to keep all of life in a perspective that maintains human relationships at a value level at least as high as that of an inanimate object. Athletes pay great attention to physical conditioning; the better athletes realize that achievement over the ordinary comes from mental conditioning as well. Managers who abuse their minds and bodies cannot expect to be effective controllers of their business, family, or social affairs.

More is learned each day about the health effects of personal excesses in terms of diet or substance abuse and of lack of exercise, rest, or recreation for physical bodies. Health care executives must have a commitment to keep healthy. They are indeed what they put into their bodies and must deal with the results of that input. Personal habits such as excesses or addictions, regardless of their type, will reap the same reward—stress.

The need to maintain a balanced personality is as great as, or greater than, maintaining a balanced checkbook. In addition to developing good health habits of balanced diet; abstinence from tobacco, drugs, and other harmful substances; moderation with alcoholic beverages; and at least a minimum amount of exercise, executives must develop good mental health habits.

The prayer of St. Francis of Assissi—"O Lord, grant me the serenity to accept those things I cannot change, courage to change the things I can, and wisdom to know the difference"—was truly prophetic for this age. St. Francis could not have foreseen the stresses of the modern-day organization, but he certainly understood the principles of a balanced personality.

To cope with stress, executives must learn to live within the parameters of their surroundings. Constant anger, pent-up emotions, inability to deal with certain people (spouse or child, physician or technician) can only build deeper and greater anger, hostility, and frustration that exhibit themselves in stressful behavior patterns. When managers first become aware of personal distress signals—anger, fear, or frustration—they should take a break and try to analyze the true source of distress as objectively as they would analyze a business problem, then take measures to reduce the stress or adjust. Recognizing where stress is coming from and trying then to deal with it at the source can prevent inappropriately and indiscriminately dumping anger or scapegoating. It is all too easy to transfer personal-relationship frustrations to the work scene or vice versa. The effects of personal conflicts in interactions with others play a large part in the struggle for mental well-being.

If executives are to live with any degree of understanding and peace of mind with themselves, notwithstanding the desire to share their lives with someone else, with the resultant complexities, it is imperative that they come to grips with several sets of issues. Introspection is difficult, but if it is to be helpful they must be as objective and as absolutely honest with themselves as possible. Here is a challenge—a simple but effective set of self-examinations: Executives should analyze, define, and understand the person they really are.

1. List their five most important personal goals in order of their importance.
2. List their five best personal characteristics.
3. List their five weakest personal characteristics.
4. List five personality characteristics they like best in other people.
5. List five things they dislike most in other people.
6. List five forms of entertainment or recreation they most enjoy.
7. List five characteristics that best represent their religious beliefs.
8. List five actions that they classify as immoral or sinful.
9. Analyze a week of their time and record how they spend their most precious resource; list the activity and the amount of time involved and calculate the percentage of the 168 hours in the week spent in that activity.

This exercise can reveal many previously unrecognized or acknowledged facts that executives might not have even thought about. However, if they are truly honest in their answers, they will have a pretty good basis for a profile of who they really are. This concept can be extended to a list for relationships with others, identifying what managers believe to be true about someone else. Of course, that requires that executives be able to listen to evaluations of themselves.

After the listing comes the hard part. Executives must be able to accept themselves as they find themselves to be—both strengths and weaknesses. Regardless of one's religion, keeping a copy of St. Francis's prayer in sight helps.

Being able to cope with themselves and translating that into relations with others brings executives to a critical point: dealing in adult characteristics as they act, react, and interact with others. So many "how-to" books have been published explaining how to achieve a balanced personality, that it is difficult to single out one without fear of failure to include other appropriate references. However, one publication that has been of particular importance to the author is *I'm OK—You're OK* by Thomas A. Harris. This has all the basic ingredients to allow individuals to gain insight enough to understand their own personal behavior and how it affects the conduct of others. This book, with its special definition of the "child-parent-adult" components of all personalities, is a helpful and liberating formula for mature interaction with others.

Executives need to know first who they are; second, what their goals and objectives are for the short term and the long term; and third, they must have dealt with the parent-adult-child adjustment triangle as defined in *I'm OK—You're OK* and become adult in all of their relationships, including family and work.

Health care executives must be unequivocally committed to a feeling that they are in the right occupation. They should enjoy all of the particular job relationships and should look forward to going to work each morning. If that one fact is not present, stress problems will be the inevitable result. Executives must be as "called" to administer the health care institution as the minister is to preach and the teacher to teach.

Persons trying to live different roles in each phase of life also will have to deal with the increased stress of the conflicting facets of life. Executives cannot afford a less rigorous mental, physical, and spiritual conditioning process if they are to deal adequately with all the stress factors they face.

PERSONAL THOUGHTS FOR THE EXECUTIVE

A few other thoughts reflect the author's personal philosophy of trying to cope in a health care institution on a daily basis. These thoughts are random, and no claim is laid for any particular source except that of living the experience described.

There is no hope for fewer stress factors in the future since society continues to wind itself tighter and tighter into that ever-narrowing spiral. Health care executives must learn to cope with stress or be destroyed by it. They must know how to analyze their environment and identify the stress factors that cause the most difficulty, then find appropriate solutions and thereby reduce their impact. Those who constantly fight surrounding circumstances and who are unable to accept the unchangeable will grow more embittered and more stressed. The author's suggestions are that executives should:

- Keep up to date with the information available; learn how to absorb it without having to study it in detail.
- Hire qualified people who understand stress and who are compatible with the managers' own personality and corporate life style.
- Delegate to other members of the organization without jealousy, greed, or fear.
- Delegate to other members of the management team the segments, departments, or divisions of the organization that the manager enjoys managing most. Delegation of responsibilities for which the executive has an inherent propensity frees the executive to concentrate on the remaining components of the business. If, for example, an executive has a strong educational or experiential background in accounting and finance, those duties can be delegated to another member of the management team with greater organizational efficiency. The executive saves time and effort because it takes less time to review and evaluate results from the delegated areas because of their familiarity.

  Managers have a tendency to act in reverse manner in this matter. They are faced constantly with the temptation to delegate the segments of the business that they dislike most or that are most difficult for them to manage. Again, the manager should delegate those areas for which they have a natural affinity. Then the manager can concentrate time and effort to those segments of the organization that are harder to manage. This structure gives a more balanced effort from management and serves the organization more favorably. It should, in the end, provide greater benefit.
- Keep the organization simple, with as few layers as possible between the top and bottom levels of employees. Do not create a situation in which the organization runs on paper or create an unnecessary, inefficient, and expensive bureaucracy.
- Use direct verbal communication as the prime management tool with associates at all levels of the institution as well as in the broader community.
- Subordinate personal recognition. It has been said that anyone can accomplish anything so long as they are willing to give someone else the credit. That is particularly appropriate for health executives.
- Select hobbies that produce something tangible—gardening, needlepoint, building, or similar activities. Do not engage in hobbies that are of the same stress and competitive level as the job.
- Put people first. Health care administration is a people business, with managers trying to get people to deliver care to other people. So, don't forget the basic goal.

In summary, health care executives can expect great changes to occur with greater frequency in their lives. It is possible to cope with those changes through preparation and understanding. They must keep in mind that health administration has stress dimensions and facts different from the usual business enterprise.

It is important for health care managers to maintain a balanced life style to help compensate for the stresses they encounter each day. Although it is difficult, it is possible to cope in the health care business and to succeed in delivering services that are beneficial to others.

It is to be hoped that the thoughts and ideas presented here help executives avoid the prescription described in the first sentence of this chapter.

BIBLIOGRAPHY

Harris, Thomas A. *I'm OK—You're OK.* New York: Harper & Row, Publishers, Inc., 1967.

Herd, J. Alan. "Cardiovascular Response to Stress in Man." *Annual Review of Physiology* 46, (1984):177–85.

Schindler, Barbara A. "Stress, Affective Disorders, and Immune Function." *Medical Clinics of North America* 69, no. 3 (May 1985):585–97.

Toffler, Alvin. *Future Shock.* New York: Random House, Inc., 1970.

———. *The Third Wave.* New York: William Morrow & Co., Inc., 1980.

Westbury, Stuart. "Management Adjustments in Changing Times." *Administrative Radiology* 4, no. 8 (August 1985):19–21.

Effecting Cooperation

Boone Powell, Jr.

7

Fundamentally, there are only two ways of coordinating the economic activities of millions. One is central direction involving the use of coercion—the technique of the army.. . . The other is voluntary cooperation of individuals—the technique of the marketplace.

Milton Friedman[1]

Historically, industry has used cooperation to advance common objectives of competing business factions. Cooperation in its truest form cannot be used by an organization simply to divert a crisis or accomplish a passing objective. Cooperation is more than pulling together; ancient galley slaves pulled together at their oars but they did not cooperate. In similar fashion, cooperation works best when competing interests *voluntarily* team together to achieve objectives. While cooperation in its purest sense can achieve many advantages that single institutions cannot accomplish by themselves, cooperative efforts with suppliers or competitors could potentially result in violations of antitrust regulations. Therefore, considerable discretion should be exercised before participation in such joint ventures.

The traditional health care industry thrived on one level of cooperation as a method of producing services in the local community. Communities offered strong support for hospitals as they worked together to meet local health care needs. The new health care industry characterized by competition, fragmentation, and increasing specialization has an even greater need for cooperation. This cooperation must result from linkages at all levels: provider to provider, provider to employer, provider to community, provider to physician, and the list continues. Health care survival and success hinge on finding the balance between cooperation and competition.[2]

WHY COOPERATION?

The first question when speaking of cooperation is: Why is cooperation important? Several factors in the new health care industry necessitate the further development of cooperation.

Competition

Perhaps the most important reason why cooperation is necessary is that competition mandates it. The experience curve or institutional learning curve has been replaced by a concept called the "health care survival curve."[3] The survival curve is embodied in the concept that competition, cooperation, and regulation are not mutually exclusive but must be balanced. Lee Iacocca explained this balance in discussions regarding Japanese automakers: "We shouldn't get mad at them; we should try to imitate them through cooperation between management, labor and government.. . . We all have to have a lot more cooperation without affecting competition."[4]

The survival curve dictates that survival and success increase as health care organizations selectively enter into cooperative ventures for mutual competitive advantage. During competitive times, cooperation becomes a growth industry. Cooperative ventures often allow companies to obtain expertise in market segments in which they could not compete otherwise.

Increasing Interdependence

A second major factor supporting cooperation is the increasing interdependence on differing segments of health care to enable the industry to deliver a successful product. Historically, health care entities simply relied on the physician referral system and government reimbursement to perpetuate their business. Today, many and various business segments are necessary to achieve success.

For example, health care growth threatens industries' ability to generate reasonable profits because of the cost of care; when industry and health care survival become intertwined and contradictory, cooperation becomes the key to accepted growth in both sectors. In similar fashion, management cannot unilaterally produce a marketable medical program without physician support, and health care products cannot be delivered without physician-hospital support, hospital-employee support, community acceptance, government blessing, trustee involvement, and a host of other interdependent segments.

Trend Toward Multihospital Systems

A third reason involves multihospital development and growth. Jeff Gold-smith has attributed the growth of multihospital systems to a trend of increasing interinstitutional cooperation; most multihospital systems must manage many institutional relationships to link health resources together in coordinated fashion.[5]

Multihospital systems are composed of a number of specialty products, departments, and skills. Because of the diversity of operations, large systems must rely on cooperation to reduce fragmentation and coordinate services. Specialty departments operate in highly defined domains and need cooperation within a system to achieve results. The greater the number of specialists and specialty departments, the greater the need for cooperation to deliver quality health care.

Innovation and Problem Solving

The fourth major reason is to enhance innovation and problem solving. Innovation requires collaborative internal and external relationships. Different segments have specific problem-solving styles and often conflicting views on how to develop new health care products. Cooperative efforts are necessary to ensure that these entities maximize expertise and devise the best methods of delivery. Cooperation ensures that all important voices regarding health care are heard and help the industry to develop customer-designed services.

Protection

The final reason why cooperation is important to health care delivery is to protect against the action of other cooperative ventures. As Peter F. Drucker stated, the balance between cooperation and competition is delicate.[6] Competitors in the health care industry also are forming cooperative arrangements and networking with employers, consumers, and insurance providers. Cooperation in the voluntary health care sector can compete more effectively against the proprietary industry to deliver services.

Milton Friedman stated that the voluntary cooperation of individuals is the technique of the marketplace.[7] Certainly, cooperation at all levels—government, the health industry, business, customers, providers, physicians, and a host of other segments—is necessary to achieve integrated care. Cooperation provides each participant with a sense of ownership and pride and benefits the health care industry in providing services to customers.

HOW COOPERATION?

Effecting cooperation in the health care field presents executives with a unique set of circumstances in one of the most complicated organizational structures in existence today: the hospital and/or health system. Professional management consultants have noted for years the intricacies of the typical hospital as to the interplay of professional, technical, and nontechnical personnel—the support services, such as food, engineering, housekeeping, and laundry; the high-tech people and functions, such as laboratory specialists and medical imaging specialists; and the full spectrum of nursing care.

To this organizational blending effort is added a group of experts highly trained and motivated, and generally independent-action oriented rather than group-action oriented: the medical staff. The physicians come into organizations that in most cases they do not own and give orders and instructions to employees they do not employ. In his years of health care management, the author has yet to see an organizational chart capture the real sense and flavor of the typical hospital. It is somewhat astounding that it functions as well as it does.

It is in this context, then, that the essentials of effective cooperation are discussed, particularly in light of the tremendous and rapid restructuring process that is occurring in the health industry.

Management Staff

Developing a sense of purpose, mission, commitment, enthusiasm, and unity within the management staff is essential to having a winning team. It is almost elemental to suggest that cooperation—a cooperative spirit and attitude toward the purposes of the organization and the participants—is required; however, assumptions such as these can lead to disappointment and ineffectiveness. All the members of the management team must be in the same boat and rowing in the same direction.

One successful way of accomplishing this is through management's involvement in the strategic planning process. Perhaps too frequently, health care institutions have left planning to outside consultants or to their own planning departments, which have produced detailed reports and presented recommendations. All too often these documents are shelved with a false sense of security that there now exists a three-to-five-year plan and that the long-range plans are worthwhile. The real issue today is that strategic planning can be done principally only by those closest to the enterprise. Although input should be sought from other key contributors, such as department heads, physicians, and trustees, the top management staff is best prepared to deal with the strategic issues of the organization.

This process usually involves a period of six to nine months and necessitates discipline from the chief executive officer through the top management team. The initial meeting with the management team ideally occurs in a retreat setting. This type of environment, plus the absence from the workplace, permits the staff to focus quality time on the issues at hand. It also creates a climate for team building.

The strategic planning process deals with three basic questions:

1. Where are we?
2. Where do we want to go?
3. How do we get there?

The chief executive officer must truly desire the frank and open discussion of the staff members in order to obtain the best results. Without this support, the process is doomed and minimal team building occurs.

The author's first encounter with strategic planning came in the late 1970s and required nine months. The first one-week retreat dealt with the following questions:

1. Where are we?
   a. Assessment
      • strengths
      • weaknesses
      • opportunities
   b. Identification of key issues
   c. Environmental assessment

2. Where do we want to go?
   a. Mission statement
   b. Goals
3. How do we get there?
   a. Action plans
   b. Implementation schedule.

The planning results from this initial effort led to an agreed-upon assessment of strengths and weaknesses, a clarification of the mission statement, and the identification of 71 action plans to enhance the strengths, fill the gaps, and evaluate and develop new opportunities. The development of the action plans involved employees, physicians, trustees, and management in the specific areas in which they could make the greatest contributions.

The organizational results were remarkable. Not only was a road plan developed for the hospital, but excitement and enthusiasm for the plan permeated the entire staff. It might legitimately be asked why people reacted this way. The response is that the process had brought about "their" plan. They helped create and develop it and, in fact, they assumed "ownership" of it. A sensing of ownership seems to result in the following:

• excitement
• motivation
• teambuilding

• cooperative spirit
• minimal turf issues
• a winning attitude.

This process has been detailed for one simple purpose—to show that it has proved successful in obtaining cooperation from and with the author's management team. Owning a "piece of the future" motivates and develops a cooperative spirit better than anything else the author knows in management.

Board of Trustees

Many executives work for and relate to boards of trustees. In systems, some of the boards may be advisory in nature but nonetheless represent citizens from the community and/or representatives from ownership, such as in some church hospitals. The need for management to earn the respect, and therefore the support and cooperation, of board members is imperative. This is particularly true when the pace of change is fast and decisions often must be made more quickly than in the past.

Based on working for a board for a number of years, and on having observed these same trustees on other nonprofit and community boards, several conclusions emerge:

- Hospital boards want to be supportive of the institution and cooperative with management.
- Hospital boards feel free to act in this manner when they believe they are informed about the organization and when the financial structure is on a sound basis.
- Hospital boards want to know that employees are treated fairly and that management's relationship with the medical staff is acceptable.
- Hospital boards want to know that management is committed to the purposes and the mission of the institution.

There are several methods of building relationships with hospital boards that can foster the kind of support and cooperation desired by management. Some that have proved successful include:

- Board retreats. This is a technique used by many in the field today. A retreat provides a forum for new ideas and concepts, program development, policy formulation of key issues, review and approval of strategic imperatives, and review of current information on both the industry and the institution. In many instances the retreat forms the basis for work in the next year.
- Board of trustees/medical board retreat. Inviting key medical staff leaders to join with the board provides a forum for exploring factors that affect both the physicians and the hospital. Outside speakers can

be extremely helpful in the educational process that must take place. Relationships among trustees, physicians and management often are enhanced.

- Educational seminars. Inviting and escorting trustees to seminars, such as those presented by the Estes Park Institute in Englewood, Colorado, represent an investment in behalf of the institution. The author has worked for two hospital organizations and has taken trustees to numerous meetings. Virtually all experiences have been rated positive by the trustee participants.

- Respect for trustees' other obligations. It is easy for executives to get so caught up in the organization that they come to expect the same time commitment from trustees. This expectation can be unfair to the trustees and can dampen their enthusiasm for the job.

- Appreciation. Showing appreciation for a board can produce remarkable results. Small remembrances at religious holidays, the inclusion of spouses at seminars and retreats, and the respect of their time go a long way in designing a cooperative spirit between a board and its staff.

This should be a primary focus for management. The changes in the health care environment, the conversion to a competitive industry, the liability exposure of trustees, the sticky problems developing in society such as abortion, etc., and the fact that too many chief executive officers are losing their jobs and being blamed for factors such as a decrease in patient days, etc., that many times are not in their control, necessitates information, communication, and time with trustees to enable them to grasp the large picture and how it is having an impact on their institutions.

Employees

If executives take the position of dictators, then cooperation from employees is unimportant. Of course, current management teachings have proved that this approach is ineffective in most cases. Hospital organizations have their cultures, values, traditions, and history that have created the fiber that weaves them together, with the common purpose of serving the patient as the strongest bond.

However, distractions such as cost cutting, productivity, insecurity, loyalty to the profession and/or union rather than the institution, and general concern for the future have placed a great deal of pressure on employees, the facility, and management. All indications point to developing a new culture in health care, a quality/value approach. Pricing sensitivity, alternative delivery systems, managed care programs, and restructuring are creating stresses for the industry.

One prominent airline executive said that when deregulation arrived his company was forced to make major changes in the way it did business.[8] It sold older and less fuel-efficient aircraft for new and more cost-effective planes. It trimmed fixed costs and established more variable costs. It had layoffs and created a two-tier pay system for new employees. All of these measures were successful. The area of the most difficulty was changing the corporate culture. Through regulation, the airline had had protected routes and, thereby, modified competition. It had to be reoriented to think and act in a competitive industry, and it proved to be the most demanding part of the transition.

The health care industry also has changed from a totally regulated industry to a competitive and deregulated one. Management is under pressure to make changes within the institution, which has placed a strain on many organizations and their employees. Cooperation from employees in this period of change is essential. To develop this cooperative spirit, executives should:

- Conduct seminars and reorientation sessions for department heads and middle managers regarding the changes in the organization and why they have occurred.
- Schedule periodic facilitywide meetings of all employees with the chief executive officer and senior management to clarify the hospital's actions and to answer questions and concerns.
- Involve sensing groups of employees to help them find solutions to problems. As an example, let employee groups determine how their work assignments should be allocated to achieve maximum productivity with the given full-time equivalent requirement.
- Establish fair policies toward the welfare of the employees if job categories are eliminated or layoffs are required. Some management staffs and institutions have lost credibility because of perceived unfairness.
- Enlist and engage employee participation in cultural change, such as guest relations programs.
- Refine new-employee orientation to meet the expectations of the institution in a competitive environment.

Employees still are the institution's most important asset and should not be taken for granted. Including them in problem solving at the level closest to them and attempting to create a sense of ownership of the institution will help bring about the cooperation needed to make the organization effective under the new rules of the game.

Medical Staff

There is probably no other area in health care management as sensitive and potentially volatile as medical staff relations. The restructuring of the health delivery system is affecting practitioners in much the same way as the hospital. Their concerns and often paranoid feelings are just as real as management's. Their life styles are being threatened and many are trying to respond in fragmented ways. Some have benefited and some have been exploited by new players in health care such as venture capitalists. The factor of resistance to change, along with feelings of frustration and anger, makes it a challenging time for management. The need to achieve cooperation is fundamental to the inherent interest of both physicians and hospitals. Some approaches for management in effecting cooperation with the medical staff include:

- Send the message to physicians that the new environment necessitates new relationships.
- Obtain concurrence from the board of trustees to enter into new partnerships with the medical staff.
- Establish and practice the win/win philosophy with physicians.
- Create joint venture opportunities with the medical staff. Several examples at the Baylor University Medical Center are as follows:

1. health maintenance organization (HMO)—60 percent-40 percent joint venture between physicians and hospital
2. preferred provider organization (PPO)—50 percent-50 percent joint venture
3. Health System TX—a joint venture management company to operate the PPO/HMO
4. Baylor Surgicare—a six-room ambulatory surgery center with a subsidiary of Baylor as general partner and 41 surgeons as limited partners.
5. Outpatient rehabilitation centers—a general and limited partnership model.

- Market the services of the medical staff. Examples are product line management of a heart center, a cancer center, an eye service, or other such entities. These efforts create a win/win situation for both parties.
- Invite outside speakers to address the medical staff to keep the physicians current.
- Attend conferences with physicians. Baylor has had numerous physicians attend the Estes Park Institute, as well as other seminars.

- Utilize retreats for specific physician groups. Some typical retreat groups have included:

  1. Medical Board
  2. Department of Internal Medicine
  3. Department of General Surgery
  4. Heart Center
  5. Cancer Center
  6. Baylor and individual practice association (IPA) board.

The scenario in today's hospital presents the potential for serious conflict between the facility and its medical staff or the opportunity to create new and more effective partnerships with physicians that will be mutually beneficial. The arena of medical staff relations is the most critical to winning in the future and carries with it the greatest premium of cooperation in order to be successful and effective.

Community Relations

Image, reputation, and a sense of being an important part of the community generally are considered important by most health care managers. Although some have written off philanthropy, many others, including the management team at Baylor, have instigated broadly based foundations with outstanding citizens joining to help accomplish the mission. Baylor has been fortunate in having more than 80 foundation directors working with it on planning task forces, capital campaigns, and endowment campaigns. Their support has been invaluable.

There is a key to enlisting the support and cooperation of these community leaders: that hospital management will be responsible citizens, as well. In Dallas, the basis for being influential and/or powerful is not money or position; it is a willingness to work for the benefit of the city. Perhaps that is why in 1960 the author adopted an admonition by the chairman of Inland Steel Corporation that if hospital executives want the support of the community, they should support their community as well.[9] This formula will produce effective cooperation in the communities in which health care executives live.

Alliances, Affiliations, and Networking

The development of alliances among health care providers (such as American Healthcare System and Voluntary Hospitals of America) and the increasing number of affiliations and joint ventures (such as local/regional networks, HMOs, PPOs) have opened a new area for building cooperative relationships.

The essential element for a cooperative attitude is creating trust between the parties and developing win/win propositions. Management should approach these new relationships in a positive and constructive fashion and foster a cooperative spirit because these links will play a much more significant role for hospitals in the future than many think.

OPPORTUNITIES FOR THE FUTURE

This is probably the most stressful, demanding, and yet exciting era in health care in years. The industry is restructuring itself and has the opportunity to shape the system of the future. It is a time of changing economic incentives, limited resources, and new relationships. New partnerships and new alliances are developing. The industry is diversifying and adjusting, and at a rapid pace.

Executives must remember, however, that their mission still is to care for people with health needs. Boards, physicians, employees, colleagues, and management still are fundamental to the process. What is changing is the structure and the mix of how the mission will be carried out. In so doing, executives must maintain that winning attitude, that cooperative spirit that not only will permit them to succeed but that also will enable them to fulfill the public trust of maintaining health care at its finest.

NOTES

1. Milton Friedman, *Capitalism and Freedom* (Chicago: University of Chicago Press, 1962).
2. Irwin Miller, *The Health Care Survival Curve* (Homewood, Ill.: Dow Jones-Irwin, 1984), viii.
3. Ibid., 2.
4. Ibid.
5. Ibid.
6. Peter F. Drucker, *Men, Ideas, and Politics* (New York: Harper & Row, Publishers, Inc., 1971), 179.
7. Friedman, *Capitalism.*
8. Personal conversation with author.
9. Friedman, *Capitalism.*

BIBLIOGRAPHY

Friedman, Milton. *Capitalism and Freedom.* Chicago: University of Chicago Press, 1962.
Miller, Irwin. *The Health Care Survival Curve: Competition and Cooperation.* Homewood, Ill.: Dow Jones-Irwin, 1984.
Sheldon, Alan, with Susan Windham. *Competitive Strategy for Health Care Organizations.* Homewood, Ill.: Dow Jones-Irwin, 1984.
Richardson, Gerald. *ABC of Cooperatives: A Handbook for Consumers and Producers.* New York: Longmans, Green and Company, 1940.

Effective Meetings

David A. Gee and Carol D. Teig

8

Meetings are the common currency of people everywhere in their business and social transactions. Speaking to a neighbor over the back fence, Stanley's confrontation with Livingston, and the presidential State of the Union address to the joint houses of Congress all represent meetings.

William Congreve observed, "When people walk hand in hand, there is neither overtaking nor meeting."[1] It is rare, however, in a complex world that individuals are so congruent in their ideas and goals that they can avoid these human interchanges. Meetings can range from casual and informal to complex and highly structured activities. Witness the elaborate preparations sometimes involving a year or more of advanced planning for a summit meeting of heads of state.

BASIC PURPOSES OF MEETINGS

In the commercial world, meetings are frequent and are an essential part of doing business. For some aggressive business leaders, a meeting may be the device in which dicta are pronounced. In participative management organizations, meetings represent two-way communication with give-and-take by all attendees.

Meetings may be called for the purpose of providing information, educating, developing policies and procedures, carrying out certain regulatory and legal requirements, fulfilling fiduciary responsibilities, performing technical control functions, developing planning and strategy, and making decisions.

Peters and Waterman in their book *In Search of Excellence,* stress the kind of spontaneous exchanges that can occur in impromptu meetings among creative people given a free rein.[2] They cite the philosophy of "management by walking around" as a device for senior managers to obtain and retain the flavor of the organization.

101

Meetings are so frequent and so popular that they also become confused with coffee klatches and bull sessions and the exchange of anecdotal war stories retold for the sheer joy of reminiscing about times gone by.

Meetings often are held for frivolous or inappropriate purposes. Peter F. Drucker notes that a symptom of poor organization is "too many meetings attended by too many people." He does add that there are certain top-level committees that do their work only in the form of meetings "but these are exceptions—deliberative organs which do not have operating functions and as a rule do not have decision-making functions either. They are organs to guide, to reflect, to review—and perhaps the most important function is to compel the operating top managers who sit down with the committee to think through their own directions, their own needs and their own opportunities." He comments that executives who spend more than a quarter of their time in meetings probably have jobs that are not clearly defined or have not been structured large enough, and they have not been made truly responsible for their function.[3]

Parkinson's first law states: "Work expands so as to fill the time available for its completion."[4] The proverbial phrase "it is the busiest man who has time to spare" also is true of the meeting process. For example, one organization regularly allows two full days for its board meetings and if the sessions end before the allotted time, executive insecurity sets in. Thus, a premium is placed on finding a chairperson who will adequately fulfill Parkinson's law.

For those who have any experience with meetings, it will be observed that the length of the session is inversely proportional to the importance of the subject. Thus a corporate board faced with a $50 million decision generally will consume no more than 15 minutes while the Boy Scout Committee will spend not less than four hours debating where next Saturday's hike should take place. As Parkinson has noted, "the total effort that would occupy a busy man for three minutes all told, may in this fashion leave another person prostrate after a day of doubt, anxiety, and toil."[5]

Parkinson goes on with some pithy observations about committee activity, especially those who attend, whom he describes as follows:

A. Those who have failed to master any one of the memorandums written in advance and showered weeks beforehand on all those who are expected to be present.
B. Those who are too stupid to follow the proceedings at all. These are readily distinguishable by their tendency to mutter to each other, "what is the fellow talking about."
C. Those who are deaf. They sit with their hands cupping their ears growling "I wish people would speak up."

D. Those who were dead drunk in the small hours and have turned up (heaven knows why) with a splitting headache and a conviction that nothing matters either way.

E. The senile whose chief pride is in being as fit as ever—fitter indeed than a lot of these younger men; "I walked here," they whisper, "pretty good for a man of 82, what?"

F. The feeble who have weakly promised to support both sides and don't know what to do about it. They are of two minds as to whether they should abstain from voting or pretend to be sick.[6]

In busy corporate life, effective organizations do not have the luxury of misusing meetings. Meetings are held for specific purposes. These purposes can be achieved when meetings are organized and conducted effectively. Choice of subject matter, participants, location, date and time, meeting logistics, and meeting strategies all become crucial to successful outcomes. It is worthwhile to examine some of these characteristics in more depth.

Types of Meeting Holders

Meetings held by formally organized groups such as standing committees (ordained by corporate bylaws) or legislative bodies (ordained by the electorate) generally have highly prescribed functions and duties. In the case of health care organizations, the Joint Commission on Accreditation of Hospitals (JCAH) mandates that formal committees be established for quality assurance, utilization review, credentials evaluation, and clinical conduct. The transactions of these bodies become the basis by which hospitals can fulfill prescribed standards.

The regulatory influence on hospitals, strongly influenced by federal standards for participation in Medicare and Medicaid and by the JCAH requirements, requires all too numerous standing committees that need preparation, time commitment from the participants, and elaborate documentation. These required structures, however, should not be confused with the strategic management functions of the organization. Peters and Waterman emphasize repeatedly that excellent companies are "vast networks of informal open communications; the intensity of communications is unmistakable in the excellent companies."[7]

On the other hand, most institutional meetings are carried forth by committees organized for specific purposes and to fulfill specific tasks. Indeed, many such committees are referred to as task forces, the implication being that once the particular mission (task) is fulfilled, the group moves on to some other activity without being perpetuated. Whatever name is applied, the charge to or goal of the committee needs to be established clearly since it is difficult for a meeting group to deal in abstraction.

Meeting Logistics

Meeting logistics can be important. Everything from size and accessibility of the meeting room, comfort (or lack thereof), the chairs, availability of refreshments, chalkboard, projection equipment, and seating arrangement all can be important factors. In relatively informal meetings, participants may seat themselves in an entirely ad lib fashion (viz., a person who refuses to face a lighted window or, conversely, a man who refuses to sit with his back to the door—shades of Wild Bill Hickok!).

In more structured meetings, especially where there are political issues that need to be resolved, seating becomes crucial. Union organizing sessions find management on one side of the table and the union on the other—in short, a direct confrontational relationship. The same is true in the demilitarized zone between North and South Korea, with the daily meetings at Panmunjam. In these sessions, not only is seating important but proper preparation is crucial. Anyone leaving the table suffers an immediate loss of face. After a six- or seven-hour session, good control of hunger, thirst, and other bodily functions is essential.

Still other meetings may be carefully crafted in advance by the placement of name cards to indicate where the participants will sit. This gives the chair the opportunity of controlling protocol and personal interactions. For example, on one board of directors, all of the outside directors are at the head end of the table where the chair sits while the inside directors are at the foot of the table, the implication being that the outside directors hold some kind of honored position, clearly a subliminal form of flattery. On the other hand, some corporations carefully intersperse inside and outside directors. This has the advantage of permitting members to get to know one another better. This can help the flow of information during the meeting between inside and outside directors but it also enables the insiders to apply pressure and attempt to control the outsiders.

The shape of the conference table frequently becomes an issue. At the first organizational meetings of the United Nations in San Francisco following World War II, seating was a major problem. The first Strategic Arms Limitation Talks (SALT) spent as much time on the shape of the table as on substantive issues. The Yalta Conference was held at a round table so that no one of the leaders would take precedence. Purely aside from these political considerations, table shape can be important, especially when it influences the ability to hear and see what is going on. Elliptically shaped tables and, in other fields, Saarinen arches and truncated pyramids, all have their advocates.

The Chair

In conducting the meeting, the chair must maintain control over events without appearing to be overly prescriptive or dominating so that the presider inhibits participation. Lefton, Buzzata, and Sherberg suggest a five-step approach aimed at improving fruitful two-way communication:

1. Arouse interest of the group by accurately describing the mission of the meeting. Proper stage setting is essential to good receptivity.
2. Further enhance receptivity by obtaining views from the other meeting participants.
3. It is only after the other meeting participants have expressed their views that the chairman expresses his own views.
4. To the extent that committee participants and/or the chairman have differing views, there needs to be a period of debate to vent emotions and resolve disagreements.
5. Final resolution with an appropriate action plan.[8]

While spontaneous meetings may be loosely structured, the more formalized mandatory meeting functions need a predictable organization. Standing committees as decreed by regulatory bodies or the organization's own bylaws will need members, a chair, and a secretary. The chair has the responsibility of directing the meeting, making sure that it is progressing in a productive fashion, keeping it focused on the issues, generally stimulating appropriate discussion, and terminating the session when its mission has been fulfilled.

Meetings ought to start on time, a maximum time commitment should be identified (an hour and a half should be the absolute maximum; the brain, voice, and seat all succumb simultaneously at that milestone), and they should end on or before the agreed deadline. Presiders who permit meetings to start late will find that participants recognize this and thus arrive late. The chair must start on time even if key participants are not present, to convey the message that discipline prevails. Adhering to an adjournment time also ensures that key players will not walk out prematurely.

In this era of feminist debate, there are some who favor the term chairwoman or chairperson; most authorities would concur that the "man" portion of chairman describes a person rather than indicating gender. It generally is wise to let the persons running the meetings to select their own appellation. It has been interesting to note that after a five-year trend toward the feminine form that the pendulum has begun to swing back to the functional title.

Effective executives insist that the meeting serve the contribution to which they have committed themselves. "A meeting called . . . to stimulate thinking and ideas . . . is a challenge . . . to everybody in the room. [The effective executive] always . . . goes back to the opening statement and then relates the final conclusions to the original intent." Contribution is key. "Focusing on contribution turns one of the inherent weaknesses of the executive's situation—his dependence on other people, his being within the organization—into a strength. It creates a team."[9]

During this process, the chair has an obligation to control the garrulous, draw out the silent, and protect the weak.[10]

In this day of outcome-oriented meetings, substance takes priority over form. Nevertheless, in some meetings form indeed becomes important, especially if there is wide divergency in viewpoints. There are several rule-books governing meeting conduct, the most familiar of which is *Robert's Rules of Order*. Full strategies develop around such rules, with legislative bodies being adept at their use. Such rulebooks also are favored by PTA groups and sewing circles since they lend a sense of drama to otherwise pedestrian undertakings. Busy executives seeking consensus within their own organizations are likely to eschew such devices. Whether or not the chair uses formal rules in running the meeting, it is worthwhile to read such a rulebook since it tends to categorize meeting events in a reasonably tidy order, which frequently can favorably affect the chair's conduct.

The Secretary

If the chair is the strategic controller of the meeting, the secretary handles tactical and logistical elements. Those who would demean the role of the secretary overlook the absolutely crucial nature of this function in making the meeting go properly. From adequate and timely notice of the meeting to the production of minutes of the events that took place, there are numerous intervening steps.

If a meeting is worth calling, it ought to include the individuals who are deemed essential for its success. Chances for good participation are enhanced by the secretary's anticipating the need for a meeting well in advance (preferably three to four weeks as a minimum), polling members as to their availability, and confirming the arrangements with a notice that provides the name of the meeting, date, time, and location, and a brief statement of the purpose or issues involved.

For meetings that are required on a regular basis, setting up the schedule a year in advance ensures that busy people will mark the date on their calendars. A reminder notice can then be sent. A return postcard is a convenient device for identifying the attendees. Where the meeting is to review complex issues, background papers are useful. They are most effective when they are sent with the notice of the meeting but certainly not less than four or five days beforehand so the participants have adequate time to read the material.

The meeting agenda is the responsibility of the chair and the secretary. It should identify the subject(s) (and designate the individual responsible for making the presentations). Some organizations specify the amount of time allotted to the subject so that a schedule can be maintained. This usually is not essential if the chair has established good discipline within the committee.

Essential actions by the secretary include reserving a meeting room and making arrangements for projection equipment, chalkboards, easels, scratch paper, and food service. To those who regard such matters as mundane and prosaic, it is only necessary to witness the unproductive chaos that results when the attendees arrive to find that the meeting place was not confirmed or that it is impossible to receive essential information because the projection equipment has broken down. Experienced committee secretaries know and understand that confirmation of all elements is essential. Simply sending a requisition or making a phone call does not ensure performance. Meetings that go off without a hitch are the result of meticulous and painstaking effort. After all, the whole purpose is to obtain a certain desired end result. If that is achieved, all is well and good; if it is not achieved because of confusion or disgruntlement over arrangements, then everyone has wasted time and energy.

Minutes

The secretary is responsible for generating minutes of the meeting. Minutes range from one-page summaries to total transcripts. The former usually fail to describe what happened while the latter are a ponderous display of what may have been an already ponderous meeting. Robert Townsend is an advocate of weekly staff meetings that provide information, take place regularly at the same time and same place, start and end on time, involve all of the attendees, and generate no paperwork other than a one-page set of minutes describing major events.[11] Some secretaries arrive with tape recorders, transcribe the entire amount, then slavishly attempt to pinpoint the salient features.

Minutes ought to reflect what actually happened, capturing the flavor and essence of the discussions and especially the end results without having to reduplicate every point and nuance. Minutes should be readable and interesting. They ought to be the kind of document that members can pick up a month later, before the next meeting, and quickly restore a train of thought as to actions taken. Probably even more important, those same minutes should be understandable five years later when the actions, possibly representing important financial or legal transactions, must be recalled with precision.

The essentials of minutes contain the name of the organization; the date, time, and place of the meeting; an attendance list; the body of the minutes, with action either underlined or otherwise highlighted for easy identification; the time the committee adjourned; and the signature of the secretary. Some organizations require that the chair also sign. The secretary ought to be able to generate minutes within 24 hours. Not only is timely receipt of the information important to the participants but it is easier to prepare the minutes when the events are fresh in mind. Experienced and facile minute takers produce good documentation quickly, effectively, and with the least amount of paper.

That last point is worth noting. In a busy, large, and highly departmentalized hospital having 100 or more committees, with each one generating documentary minutes for subsequent review by the JCAH, by residency review committees, by auditors, and others, it is easy to become enmeshed in oceans of paper. On the other hand, good documentation is important, especially in a litigious and regulatory society.

CONFERENCES AT RETREATS

Another kind of increasingly popular meeting event is the retreat (see also Chapter 7). Retreats should not be confused with normal meetings since they involve an entirely different level of commitment than the specific task-oriented business session. Organizations using such conferences hold them at annual, biennial, or even less frequent intervals as a means of devoting uninterrupted time to philosophic and reflective matters. A retreat generally consists of a meeting lasting a day and a half or two days in some reasonably comfortable spot away from the place of business where individuals are not interrupted by phone calls or the temptation to do competing tasks.

Major issues can be developed in depth, discussed at length, and in the course of an educational interchange a sense of direction and even consensus can be achieved. Not to be overlooked is the social interchange that can occur. Many organizations encourage the participants to work hard during the formal parts of the retreat but give ample time for recreation or relaxation. Board, medical staff, and administrative individuals who see one another only in a business setting frequently take a different view of those with whom they work when there is time for the social graces.

A word of caution about retreats: The success of these ventures frequently yields to the temptation to couple them with visits to fancy resorts. While big corporations may be able to get away with a retreat in Acapulco or Maui, cost-conscious hospitals will save public relations embarrassment by using the excellent conference centers available in many parts of the country.

AUTOMATION

Some organizations have automated the meeting process through the use of electronic voting devices. These range from fairly straightforward vote machines such as used by the House of Representatives in which all members can record their votes simultaneously. Quick tabulation is then possible and the results are displayed at once. Other companies use more sophisticated devices for forming consensus and reaching a decision. One, called the Consensor, is described by Meyer.[12] It not only provides yes/no type of information but also permits weighting or gradations of interest. The American Hospital Association Board has used a computerized device that not only records votes but creates descriptive charting of results for true cost-benefit relationships. The results are revealed quickly on a video screen and let all members know the opinions of their conferees without engaging in long and tedious debate. Where there are obvious deviations from an anticipated result, attention can be focused on gaining better understanding and consensus of important issues.

THE CONVERSE SITUATION

While meetings can be important, fruitful, productive, interesting, stimulating, and even fun, the converse also is true when the sessions become an excuse for inaction and can be dull, unproductive, boring, and a waste of time. Meetings can become the device for manipulation, intrigue, and occasionally malicious behavior. Meetings can be calm and they can be stormy:

> First Witch: When shall we three meet again?
> In thunder, lightning, or rain?
> Second Witch: When the hurly-burly's done,
> When the battle's lost and won.[13]

In the final analysis, the effectiveness of any meeting will depend not only on its planning and organization but also on the shared desire of its participants to achieve results that could not be obtained through individual decisions. Meetings can only be as productive as the executives and participants choose to make them.

NOTES

1. William Congreve, *The Double Dealer* (1694).

2. Thomas J. Peters and Robert H. Waterman, Jr., *In Search of Excellence* (New York: Harper & Row, Publishers, Inc., 1982).

3. Peter F. Drucker, *Management* (New York: Harper & Row, Publishers, Inc., 1973), 548.

4. C. Northcote Parkinson, *Parkinson's Law* (Boston: Houghton Mifflin Co., 1957).

5. Ibid.

6. Ibid.

7. Peters and Waterman, *Search*, 121–2.

8. Robert E. Lefton, V. R. Buzzata, and Manuel Sherberg, *Improving Productivity Through People's Skills* (Cambridge, Mass.: Ballinger Publishing Co., 1980).

9. Peter F. Drucker, *The Effective Executive* (New York: Harper & Row, Publishers, Inc., 1966).

10. Antony Jay, "How to Run a Meeting," *Harvard Business Review* 54, no. 2 (March–April 1976).

11. Robert Townsend, *Up the Organization* (New York: Alfred A. Knopf, Inc., 1970), 107.

12. Herbert E. Meyer, "The Meeting Goers Lament," *Fortune* (September 22, 1979): 94.

13. William Shakespeare, *Macbeth* 1.i.1.

Implementing Change

Robert C. Bills

9

Implementing change. It sounds like the simplest of statements but, in fact, denotes the most complex and difficult task an organization can undertake. The statement personifies what usually proves to be an organizational revolution. For while change is not without its rewards, it most often is fraught with hurdles that challenge even the best of management teams.

GETTING A PERSPECTIVE

Organizational change is a game that has very high stakes, both practically and politically. The players will change: often those who start the game may not be those playing at the end. It is the risk, and potentially the reward, that executives confront. Therefore, it becomes critical for an organization to determine just how much it is willing to wager, weighing the pitfalls against the possible gains. Without this evaluation, the best-laid plans can result in dismal failure: "change for only change's sake" is never fruitful or productive. And, regardless of the type of business involved, implementing change, once objectives have been identified, is both exhausting and exhilarating. It clearly gives credence to the phrase that "only the strong shall survive."

In health care, because of the industry's state of flux and turmoil, the challenge is even greater and more complex than other businesses more accustomed to market ups and downs. In health care, executives have lulled themselves into believing that they would always have the luxury of time and, with that, full control of the market and the communities served. They never even considered the idea that patients should be viewed as customers. In retrospect, that position was comparable to the assumption that nothing could, nor would, sink the *Titanic*. As a by-product of this "forward into the past" thinking, health care professionals are likely to find the implementation of change far more uncomfortable than their counterparts in any number of long-established industries (e.g., automotive, food service, pharmaceuticals, garment).

However, any discussion of implementing change, no matter what the perspective, must encompass a myriad of factors. These include ethics, planning assumptions, objectives, timing, corporate evaluation, and the importance of feedback. Nonetheless, as this analysis demonstrates, executives may find themselves recognizing that there are still other points to cover.

Since a comprehensive review of major organizational change would require an entire book, the focus here purposely is on a number of basic, essential issues. Although the examples used are specific, the concepts they illustrate can be applied universally.

As a packaged process, the implementation of change requires attention to a multitude of elements, not just those conveniently integrated or currently in vogue. The caution is that change requires an investment of time and organizational energy. Based on experience, the author doubts that it can be viewed as a short-term affair. Executives who are not prepared to consider seriously all the basic components in the implementation process might as well prepare themselves for limited success. Taking this one step further, if they are not ready to devote full attention to all aspects of the effort, change becomes nothing more than an academic exercise that will be disruptive at best.

THE ETHICS COMPONENT

It is imperative to recognize and understand that the game of organizational change is first and foremost one of people. Ethics, or moral principles, are integral components in the process and cannot be overemphasized if the effort is to prove beneficial. The question of corporate ethics creates a personal dilemma that faces every changemaker involved. While it is difficult to address this highly charged issue adequately in one chapter, it is important to comment on, even if in a limited manner.

There is an obligation on the part of the organization to define and communicate its position on ethics. The ethics embraced by the organization must be explained carefully to the changemakers, then applied consistently. Consistency of practice is the hallmark of positive results.

Coupled with communication and consistency must be opportunity: opportunity for members of the staff to respond under the new set of performance standards involved in the implementation of change (working harder, better, and longer). In health care, where managers and employees traditionally deal with ethical questions on a day-to-day basis, there may be even a heightened sensitivity to these important issues and questions.

Corporate ethics, therefore, cannot be overlooked in the implementation process for either internal or external audiences without significant negative implications and consequences. It is a factor that will have a major impact on the organization once the dust of change has finally settled.

PLANNING

Before an organization seriously considers implementing change, two important planning steps must be taken:

1. The type of change being contemplated needs to be defined. While this may be interpreted as a statement of objectives or goals, it is intended to be broader based in both scope and purpose.
2. Those involved in the preparation phase should compile a number of planning assumptions, or observations, regarding the internal and external environment. These represent variables, some of which are fixed, affecting the change process.

An understanding of both steps is essential if the effort is to prove prolific. As noted earlier, change for only change's sake usually is ineffective. It creates unrest and often is costly to an organization in terms of people and of its ability to confront environmental issues. It also is expensive from a purely dollar-and-cents (sense) perspective. Therefore, the time spent in defining the type of change desired is, in fact, time well spent.

Once it is decided what needs to be changed, there must be an evaluation to determine who or what will be affected. Is the goal to change attitudes? If so, is the target internal or external? Are the attitudes those of senior management, middle management, employees, physicians, the board, or a combination of one or more of these key groups? Are the attitudes community based? If that is the case, does that include all segments of the community (the public at large) or a specific group (e.g., the elderly, men, women)?

Simultaneously, the question must be asked, "Why didn't we attempt this change earlier?" This organizational soul-searching is important, although it may not prove to be an enjoyable experience. It does help identify the real corporate culture, which executives must come to grips with if the change is to succeed. This retrospective exercise provides a clearer picture of just what methods and tools are needed in the change process. Simply put, health care executives need to know where they were, and where they are, before they can know where they are going.

Once the type of change has been defined, they are prepared for step two: developing planning assumptions. These are internal and external environmental observations, some of which may be either fixed or constant. These assumptions influence the time of the process, the tools used to implement change, and most important, the players involved. Among the list of planning assumptions some may be so obvious that there is a tendency to ignore them. Nevertheless, despite their obvious nature, they are important and will have an impact on the change effort. Others may be so subtle that members in the organization may find them difficult to both understand and accept. However, both extremes are critical components in constructing a viable implementation plan.

An example of an *obvious external* assumption would be:

There will continue to be a shift from inpatient services to outpatient services.

An example of a *subtle internal* assumption would be:

The employees will continue to lack awareness of the necessity for change, despite media attention.

An example of a *fixed* (constant) assumption would be:

The organization will remain in the health care delivery business.

USE OF A KITCHEN CABINET

But the list is only as valuable as the people who develop it. Leaders may assess their organizational culture and the changes needed and decide that this preplanning should be done by a small, select number rather than by the organization as a whole. Depending upon the circumstances, this select group need not necessarily be restricted to senior management. Since change demands creativity (thinking outside the square) and a fresh perspective (mixed with reality), executives may find themselves launching an in-house talent search, seeking the movers and shakers, regardless of their position or rank. This "kitchen cabinet" can become the most valuable source of uncensored information. The group may consist of individuals not typically or officially viewed as leaders; however, their lack of official standing may work to the executives' advantage in functioning as excellent behind-the-scene communicators.

While executives may opt to develop a kitchen cabinet for this preplanning phase, this should not be interpreted as meaning that these are the only persons needed to be involved. Clearly, a small-group approach is the most efficient route in these early stages; however, the organization as a whole must be involved in subsequent phases if the process is to ultimately succeed. Without full participation or, better yet, the opportunity for full participation, resistance levels will increase. Employees at all levels need to feel significant in and important to the corporate culture. This involvement of the internal audience will provide a firm foundation of support once the change process is set in motion.

The approach selected must be determined on a department-by-department or unit-by-unit basis. The direction taken can be decided only after an honest and sometimes painful assessment of the organization's strengths and weaknesses. Experience dictates that without this introspective evaluation, implementation of change in any form is doomed to fail.

The discussion thus far has examined the following points:

- Organizational change is primarily one of people and carries with it a responsibility to address corporate ethics.
- Communication, consistency, and opportunity are essential.
- The change must be defined in scope as well as short- and long-range terms.
- A list of planning assumptions—that is, variables having an impact on the task of implementing change—must be compiled.
- The planning of the change process may be limited to a small, select group. However, the actual implementation of change must involve all those affected.

MAKING THE TRANSITION

It is important to separate the planning phase from the implementation process. The one deals with preparation for change and may be far more theoretical or optimistic in its overall approach. The other, implementation, is action oriented and involves detail and follow-through.

To make the transition from planning (theoretical and broad in scope) to implementation (action oriented and detail oriented), flexibility is imperative. In other words, how is it possible to make the "perfect" work in an "imperfect" setting? What happens when one or more of the planning assumptions changes in midcourse? How do executives respond when the organization does not react as projected? What should occur when key players opt to leave the corporation during a critical implementation phase? What can be done when those responsible for certain portions of the process fail to perform? Can executives, in fact, strategically anticipate the pitfalls? Can they plan spontaneity?

The answer to all these questions is twofold:

1. The executives must maintain their confidence in, and the commitment to, the process of change. It often becomes far easier to abandon the effort than to find viable solutions, especially when confronting unanticipated problems.
2. The executives must commit the organization, on a long-term and consistent basis, to a strong, integrated management development program, complete with as much cross-training as possible.

More times than not, an organization finds itself unable to continue the change process because there is no contingency plan in terms of people. However, this management development plan is not as simple as it sounds. It is not just a matter of taking all managers and scheduling them into educational courses. Just as the organization as a whole was evaluated, senior staff members must take a hard look at their own managers as to their abilities, capabilities, strengths, weaknesses, and attitudes. If the ultimate goal is to assure successful implementation and support of the change process, this evaluation exercise is essential. Realistically, one manager may have the qualities that allow for this additional management dimension while another, despite competence in one particular job, may not. It is not (always) possible to fit a round peg into a square hole.

A CASE HISTORY

Before describing the author's organization and its experience, it is helpful to have a broad view of where it was and what it is. Valley Presbyterian Hospital is in the San Fernando Valley, a suburb of Los Angeles, with a population of 1.5 million. There are 27 hospitals, varying in size and scope, within a ten mile radius. Valley Presbyterian is an independent, nonprofit, community hospital of 363 beds with a growing number of external subsidiaries.

Valley Presbyterian was established in 1958 as a community-based institution. It developed under the guidance of one of the leaders in health care, Henry X. Jackson, who served as administrator for 25 years. He made it a premier facility, expanding the physical plant and scope of services and attracting a solid, highly regarded medical staff. In 1983, Jackson chose to pursue other hospital-related interests, at which time the author was promoted to CEO.

The management team monitored the industry and knew change was essential to the hospital's future. Although it already had begun preparing for change, that effort was on more of an academic than practical level. However, the hospital faced a difficult task since it was so deeply rooted in tradition. The management team recognized and anticipated that there would be concern and discomfort among the employee population since much of the staff had a long history with the hospital. It was definitely a safe and stable environment from their perspective.

Unfortunately, there is always a certain amount of insecurity inherent in any type of change. It is part of human nature to question where the institution is going, how the change will affect job security, and what will be expected once the changes have occurred. The basic questions often become, "Where will I fit after all the changes have been implemented? Will I still have a place or a job?"

Winning Support

It is imperative that executives recognize these strong emotional reactions in choosing the implementation tools to be used. While keeping the reasons and goals of the total change effort in focus, tools should be developed that will generate awareness, support, and enthusiasm. It is important for everyone to understand why change is necessary, especially if the status quo has been satisfying. Smooth implementation is almost impossible without support from internal audiences who, in the final analysis, are the implementors of the process.

Last but not least, the degree of success for the organization will be determined by the amount of enthusiasm created by the change, once systems are in place. This component will directly affect factors such as productivity, follow-through, institutional pride, and, most important, relationships with consumers.

An entire chapter could be devoted to the subject of customer satisfaction, especially in health care. The history of the industry shows that providers seldom or never thought of patients as customers. In fact, the term is difficult for some to swallow even today. It almost sounds as though they are in the same business as a Macy's or Burger King or Chevrolet. But the truth is that the product is quality medical attention, and the patients and their families are the customers.

The difference between health care and other service-oriented businesses is the *product* and the fact that most customers *do not want* what the industry is selling. That statement is worth thinking about for a moment. People *want* new clothes. They *like* eating out. They *celebrate* the purchase of a new car. They seek those products with a positive, cheerful attitude. In the health care delivery business, the customers (patients and their families) usually are afraid, uncertain, and filled with anxiety.

As a result, the customers' emphasis on service and guest relations becomes far more serious. They scrutinize these areas intensely. Executives who doubt the validity of that position should take time and review patient questionnaires. The primary areas of complaint deal with food service (e.g., meals that are cold, delayed, or poorly prepared), ambience (e.g., room too hot or too cold or too small), and employee-patient relations (e.g., rudeness, lack of prompt response). Translated, all these items focus on customer service, an area requiring concentrated attention as change is implemented.

Where to Start

The key point to remember, considering all the facets examined thus far, is that the implementation of any change must start at the top. This is particularly difficult in the health care delivery business because of the tremendous amount of inbreeding fostered under the pretense of professionalism.

While any number of industries seek and recruit high-powered executives from a myriad of diverse backgrounds and experience, it is only recently that there has been a move to follow suit in the health care field. Most of these "outsiders" have been channeled into marketing rather than other, more traditional, health care positions. This reluctance to cross industrial lines has made health care organizations somewhat complacent and myopic in their view of, and ability to deal with, the implementation of change.

Tools of Change

At Valley Presbyterian Hospital, the situation was further complicated by the fact that the facility had been under the management of a consistent, stable group of people for many years. Add the fact that the "new" administrator had been promoted from within after ten years with the hospital and the result was an internal audience (employees, physicians, and board) whose attitude toward change and tradition was difficult to alter.

Therefore it became essential that the change process start with the CEO. This primarily involved perceptions of management style and business philosophies. It was necessary to develop a tool that not only would ensure housewide communication but also would directly influence perceptions about the author's new role as CEO. As CEO, the author not only had to activate the change process but, in fact, become a target of the very process being initiated.

To tackle this multifaceted task, the author prepared what was referred to as the State of the Union. While this may be called other things in other organizations, this was developed to coincide with the presidential address and designed with four primary objectives in mind:

1. It had to communicate clearly the new CEO's goals for the organization.
2. It had to demonstrate that the CEO felt change was essential and needed the support of the organization.
3. It had to build awareness of *why* things had to change and what would be expected.
4. It had to be tangible evidence of the new CEO's style and lay the foundation for a new image in this role.

This State of the Union could have easily been sent out as a memo or included in an annual report. However, implementing change is more than documentation, systems, evaluation, and demands. It requires strategic timing, effective presentation, and a persistent, minute focus on detail. These factors represent part of an important selling campaign that must be integrated into the process if the total effort is to succeed.

In this case, the State of the Union, or President's Address, had to be staged as a major event if the designated objectives were to be achieved. It was, after all, conveying a message regarding the importance of change. It had to make a serious and positive impression if the words were to filter down throughout the organization and become the basis for action.

With an eye to tailoring the tools of change to fit and, at the same time, modify the corporate culture, management chose to utilize the State of the Union to launch its comprehensive change process. Since this project was intended to be a presentation of philosophy that would serve as the umbrella or reference point for actual implementation, it was imperative that all parties involved (employees, physicians, and the board) hear the same message.

Therefore, the effort was organized to use all vehicles available. These included a video tape of the actual delivery, letters to the staff, distribution of the speech, and inclusion in all in-house publications. The CEO was determined to inform, educate, and facilitate mobile communication with a high degree of accuracy. The launch program could not and would not allow the rumor mill to swing into high gear.

Although this demanded time, planning, and detailed orchestration, it was recognized that it was only scratching the surface since it was philosophically based and theoretical in approach. The next step was to devise tools that would provide a smooth and effective transition from the idea and planning into the practical, action-oriented phase.

This next step required more than simple assignment of new managerial responsibilities; each party had to be assisted in revising its own professional image. In other words, if the managers were expected to be the critical link in the organizational chain and perform differently, they had to see themselves differently. And it was the top executives' responsibility to be certain that those new roles were carefully defined and outlined.

This practical application was demonstrated through a carefully developed and executed business planning program involving every department and manager in the hospital. This should not be confused with traditional strategic planning in which it is quite common to use managers as resources in obtaining broad-based information. In this process they became responsible for the functions of defining and planning as if their respective departments were separate—that is, strategic business units in and of themselves. While this approach may be traditional in other industries, with few exceptions it has not been integrated in health care. It is fair to say that entrepreneurship has not been a word frequently used or practiced in hospitals. Valley Presbyterian, through its business planning tools, attempted to introduce this concept and to foster an attitude that stepping outside the square *is* the expected norm.

The Payoff

The 1980s have become a time of reckoning for health care professionals. If the industry's facilities are to survive and prosper, executives must look to managers for more than technical expertise or length of service. Valley Presbyterian Hospital recognized that it was no longer appropriate to promote or recruit individuals without considering their business and general management ability. As competitive activity continued to exert pressures, a manager's technical ability no longer could be used as the primary criterion for corporate performance. Through the business planning program and the direct participation of all managers, it has been possible to tangibly demonstrate both what change is expected and how to meet these new expectations.

This process also provides an excellent opportunity to further evaluate the organization's strengths and weaknesses. As noted earlier, the implementation of change carries its share of risks and rewards. It may be found that some managers simply cannot adjust and, in some cases, have no desire to make the changes necessary to meet the new expectations. The other side of the coin is that change may lead to the discovery of hidden talent long overlooked by senior staff.

All in all, the business planning effort, as a major component in the implementation of change, begins as an organizational convulsion or what could be politely viewed as controlled chaos. It becomes productive only after having the opportunity to deal with attitudes and the persons involved receive some type of payoff or reward.

The payoff comes in making all the participants in the change feel that they have made a significant contribution to the organization. This must be interlinked with some tangible evidence that their contribution *has* in fact made a difference. The executive's response to their efforts and input cannot be simply a cheerleading exercise. Making participants feel significant can be accomplished only through a carefully designed system of feedback and a firmly planted approach to accountability.

Like the initiation of change, feedback and accountability must start at the top, with the CEO, and extend outward to all other senior administrators. The impact of these two issues cannot be underestimated. Yet executives may find, as Valley Presbyterian did, that these can become primary areas of weakness as change proceeds. This weakness may create a backlash of resistance (to change) among managers and severely hamper the process and subsequent results.

It would be assumed that providing feedback is so fundamental that it does not require special attention. After all, the concept is no different from a performance review, a basic management tool. However, whether it occurs in a formal or informal manner, it represents an opportunity for all participants to explore what has and has not been accomplished; in other words, basic feedback. Properly conducted, this feedback allows for mid-course adjustments and also can serve as a motivator and reinforcement of the change process itself. But, since it is such an elementary management tool, regardless of the type of business, product, or operation, many organizations fail to incorporate feedback formally into the plan for executing change.

Although feedback is easily taken for granted, experience confirms that it often is the major obstacle hindering the successful accomplishment of the stated objectives. Feedback requires a substantial investment in time. It requires senior management to adhere to tight deadlines, irrespective of other organizational responsibilities. In fact, this entire focus on feedback, the time it demands, and the additional pressure it exerts on top executives, is crucial in understanding that the role of the middle manager is not the only one being singled out for alteration. The role of the senior executive also is being modified.

If health care, as an industry, is to move forward, it must review and subsequently revise the methods by which it conducts business. Given the current turmoil and muddied predictions for the future, it no longer can afford to pay lip service to those who demand new standards in its "business" attitudes, practices, and efficiencies: the customers (patients/families), third party payers, business/industry, and the government.

However, awareness of feedback without full attention to the importance of timing is insufficient. Multidirectional communication will facilitate transition from one phase of implementation to the next, but it must be employed carefully. Poorly timed or insensitively delivered feedback will create as much damage as no feedback at all. Whether a weakness in this area exists because of a lack of senior staff commitment or unsophisticated management skill, the impact will be the same: negative credibility for top-level staff and indignation and disillusionment at lower levels as to the validity of the change itself.

ACCOUNTABILITY AND LEADERSHIP

These potential problems, in turn, raise critical issues regarding accountability and its role in the implementation plan. Experience affirms that it is next to impossible to execute change successfully without new standards of accountability within the organization. If the institution's integrity is to be preserved, all partners in the change—senior and middle managers alike—must be held responsible and accountable for their portion of the process.

This means that the initiators of change (CEOs or others) must have the courage to define guidelines of accountability and the conviction to ensure that they are activated consistently, despite any personal conflicts that it may create. By maintaining high standards of expectations, the CEO demonstrates commitment to the change process and sets a precedent that will become the foundation for future efforts.

OTHER PARTNERS

Although health care professionals have thought of themselves as different from their counterparts in other businesses, it is appropriate that as any industry is forced to respond and react to market changes, the people connected with it change as well. Health care is no exception. A discussion of the implementation of change within this industry would be incomplete without addressing the role of the medical staff and the board of directors.

To be blunt, it would be suicidal to attempt any type of major organizational change without considering the impact of—and on—the medical staff. For a hospital, it represents a key audience that can either support and enhance the change process or seriously disrupt and impair its potential benefits. This places hospital executives in a vulnerable position, since their control of these particular partners is limited.

Typically, medical staffs function as separate, independent entities. They cannot be viewed in the same context as paid employees. However, this is not to imply that the same concepts and tools are not relevant; the difference lies in the way they are applied. It is essential to recognize that corporate change both affects and is affected by the involvement and attitudes of these key stakeholders. Never before in the industry's history have issues such as loyalty, alliance, and exclusivity had more meaning for the future. Effective health care executives must intimately understand the physicians' point of reference and, through this awareness, strategically and appropriately include them in the total design of change.

None of the tools used in the Valley Presbyterian Hospital efforts are so unique as to appear revolutionary, but a slightly different approach was taken. The difference lies in the combination and execution. For instance, there was heavy reliance on retreats as a way to inform, educate, stimulate, and generate ideas. A conscious attempt also was made to practice what amounts to participatory management: involving the physicians in the planning, agenda, and presentations at these weekend meetings.

However, retreats are not and cannot be held frequently enough to maintain the momentum required in the implementation of change. Therefore, what is called the Medical Management Communications Committee (M^2C^2) was developed. Unlike other traditional committees at the hospital, M^2C^2 was created specifically as a forum in which issues, information, and concerns could be discussed openly and honestly. With its members drawn from the hospital's senior and middle management and from the medical staff, the group provides an environment for exchange that has not been possible to duplicate in any other committee.

Established in 1984 as a direct result of one of the retreats, the committee has grown in influence. Although it does not function as a policymaking group, there is no question that it has played a major role in strengthening and improving relationships among the parties. M^2C^2 also has become an invaluable conduit of information and support as the hospital and medical staff move through environmental and organizational change.

Equally important, the Medical Management Communications Committee has developed as a catalyst for change for both groups of members. It has clarified and heightened awareness that the hospital and medical staff are mutually dependent.

The third member of the health care organization's triangle is, of course, the board of directors. Along with management and the medical staff, boards are being pressed by environmental issues to review their function and then modify it to meet new demands. In relation to implementing change, some boards opt to become involved in the day-to-day operation, although that is more the exception than the rule. Most serve in an advisory capacity, providing counsel and guidance based on the collective expertise of its members.

It therefore becomes essential for the CEO to maintain open communication, providing the board with complete, concise, and accurate information. This approach, in turn, allows its members to assist the organization by making thoughtful decisions based on fact. A high degree of mutual trust must be established for policies to coincide with the organization's goals for change. Clearly, the role of the board in the implementation lies in the area of providing input and support.

EFFECTIVE LEADERSHIP

As evidenced by the number of factors discussed, implementing major organizational change is anything but easy. However, if it were possible to bottle all the elements reviewed thus far, the product label would have to read "effective leadership." While having leaders within the organization does not, and cannot, guarantee 100 percent success in the task of change, without a cadre of effective executives, it is highly improbable that corporate objectives can be accomplished.

What constitutes effective leadership? It certainly encompasses more than responsibilities or title. Health care organizations that survive and flourish in the future will require executives who are effective managers as well as corporate leaders. The mistake has been in thinking that management and leadership were synonymous.

An individual can be a good manager without being a leader but cannot be an effective leader without being a strong manager. A leader not only attends to detail, as does the effective manager, but also has a focus or vision of the future that is broad based.

In implementing change, effective leaders inspire confidence among the doers, providing the attitude and motivation that says, "the rewards outweigh the risks." Strong leadership paves the way for the organization to venture into unexplored territory, leaving the safety of the status quo behind. Effective executives, however, become the solid foundation needed for the successful implementation of change, a process that must be continuous and by definition is constantly in motion.

Implementing change. It sounds like the simplest of statements but, as demonstrated, is the most complex and difficult task an organization can undertake. Yet, despite its hurdles and its painful and taxing elements, change represents the promise of the future that rejuvenates an organization and allows it to grow and prosper.

Avoiding Common Causes of Executive Failure

Sheldon S. King

10

Executive failure often is synonymous with the firing of the chief executive officer—with the loss of a position often attained after years of service at lower managerial levels and in a particular health care organization. Clearly, such failures are not a function of years of executive experience but of a number of other factors that appear to result from the accelerated pace of change as well as the complexities of executive decision making. The fact that such turnover is not infrequent, and often comes after years of acceptable service, suggests that current causes of executive failure may differ from prior patterns. In reviewing such issues, it is assumed that this does not include failures that involve conflict of interest, fiduciary responsibility, or conduct that is unethical, immoral, or illegal.

In addition to the individual disruption and personal injury that result from the dismissal of an executive, there often are grave problems for the institution. Any momentum it has developed may come to a halt, its programs may become wasteful or ill directed, and it may seem immediately to be rudderless. These institutional problems occur even after the dismissal of an executive who has not been a strong leader but who has been, as many are, a stabilizing influence.

The morale of the facility and its workers suffers, and no matter how well justified the dismissal seems to be, it produces elevated levels of anxiety and fear among other managers and in the staff generally. It is not unusual for this to be seen as a signal to senior and middle management to find other positions. The search for an individual to replace the removed officer is in itself a disrupting experience, and the consequences of new leadership always mean changes in the executive structure and in the organization's need to conform and work with a new style of leadership.

HOSPITALS AND OTHER INDUSTRIES

Chief executives under the stress of the reregulated or competitive era in health care have much in common with those in industrial settings that turn out products as well as services. Each is required to work successfully with a board of directors, each is concerned with producing a healthy bottom line that ensures the institution's financial security and that not incidentally is a measure of executive performance, each is required to work in competition with neighboring institutions, and each constructs and works through an administrative hierarchy or management structure intended to accomplish the organization's end purposes.

In health care facilities, the product seemingly is less measurable or well defined and is difficult to compare with other institutional results. There is increasing interest and development in the area of outcome measurement for hospitals.

There are, of course, well-observed differences. In many industries, the chief executive is of the industry; it is not unusual for a computer scientist to become the manager of an organization that produces computer hardware and software. In other industries, the executive will be someone who is trained specifically for business leadership and will come out of the ranks of marketing or finance or organization. The senior technology ladder in hospitals, however, is populated by physician expertise. Only a few of them emerge as hospital CEOs.

Nonphysician hospital administrators who are responsible for the care of all patients as the agents of the board do not direct the process of care. They cannot order the most innocuous of medications or tests since they are not licensed to do so. They thus are in the position of being responsible for the activities of others whose technical expertise they cannot judge or direct specifically. Conflicts between management and the medical staff often are a direct result of the combined inability to meet on a common ground. They also tend to regard each other as advocates of opposite positions or as being directly adversarial, rather than positively.

DEFINING THE ROLE

Most executive failure stems from an inability to define the role clearly and to lead decisively, but not arbitrarily or dictatorially. It is helpful to focus briefly on managerial style or techniques, suggesting some of the conscious efforts management should make in an environment that requires leadership.

Each organization has its own cultural set, and while elements of it are common from hospital to hospital, each facility has an individual culture that differs from its neighbors. The differences are not as important as the ability to recognize that they exist and that they require identification of an organization culture that is defined in terms that the board, the medical staff, and the hospital staff accept and believe reflect accurately their perception of that culture.

As observed in 1970 by Alvin Toffler, it is not only the frequency of change but also the accelerated pace of change that requires an individual, organizational, and emotional ability to cope with that striking feature of management life.[1] One of the problems for administrators is that the need for rapid change and decision making translates into a pattern of acting without the participation of appropriate representatives of the institution's interests. Administrators need a sense of balance and understanding of which facts and participations are necessary, and recognition that too much communication is almost impossible.

In spite of the clichés that often accompany such descriptions, executive style should be open, candid, neither threatened easily nor threatening, recognizing the importance of thorough communications and focusing on management as a mutually interdependent process of groups working together. To avoid executive and institutional failure, any system of organized behavior must provide rewards for behavior that fit the facility's cultural approach to action, that allow and build in a system of intervention and correction of aberrant behavior, and that work in the CEO's absence.

The organization requires clear decision making, including specific rules and regulations governing that process. It must be more than reasonably clear who makes final decisions in terms of who has the authority to do so, what delegations have taken place for what ends in the institution, and what the role of the organization's committees should be.

There is an overwhelming tendency to appoint a committee or task force or working group or any one of a number of trend/approaches when executives wish to avoid making decisions. Committees that develop their own lives and go on in perpetuity without producing tangible and useful results are an indictment of management function. Executive style should include the appointment of one-shot or ad hoc committees rather than ones that appear sanctioned to enjoy continued life. The committee's role in the organization should be defined clearly: Is it to make a decision? Is it to recommend issues? Is it to provide a sounding board?

THE ROLE OF PLANNING

Committees should be a useful tool of management and not blamed for failure if they are used inappropriately. The institution needs a common context for its decision-making apparatus that identifies and recognizes the facility's values system and any plans on which decisions are based.

Strategic planning should become more than a gesture to match current rhetoric. It usually is overstressed, overdone, and underused. A significant failure occurs when the strategic plans, however well designed, beautifully written, and unanimously approved, simply sit on the shelf. The development of the plan itself, its process, and its constituency is key, including the advance commitment that it will be used. The chief executive officer who does not lead the development of a strategic plan and who does not select the committee members who develop that plan is inviting failure.

A major factor in the development of a strategic plan is the committee participants who formulate it; physicians acting in a proactive way are an essential ingredient. It is essential to identify the movers, the doers, the voices of criticism, the thoughtful members of the staff, not those who may be cronies of the CEO, and to induce them to become members committed actively to that process. Hospital board members must be introduced into the planning and participate as early as possible in the process; they bring strength and understanding, and legitimize the process. The presence of members of both the medical staff and of the board guarantees an understanding and exchange that is not accomplished when their roles are limited to reading reports, and where the heat of discussion and the process of compromise and adjustment is absent.

It is the responsibility of the CEO, as chairman of the strategic planning committee, to provide all of the material for the work of the group that will shape, redo, and convert it to a working document. The work must be seen as a regularized process by the physicians, who often are fearful of the economic crises in medical care as they affect them personally, and by board members, who have a fiduciary responsibility to the institution. It must be designed as an effective working tool. One approach is to regard the plan as a final draft, which implies change, revision, rethinking, reexamination, and a recommitment to what the plan contains. It provides the long view that management must be able to develop, defining the mission of the institution and providing a vision for the future.

It is that vision that will characterize the executives' stamp on the institution and from which their leadership should emerge. The tactics—the steps to get there (i.e., the marketing plan, the aggressive forward-looking approach, networking, acquisition, new services activities)—should flow from this plan, which then becomes a common source for decisions and directions in the hospital. All results must be measurable. Without active implementation, planning is futile and leaves the institution worse off than in its absence.

DECISION MAKING

Since other chapters in this book relate to communications and leadership, a focus on decision making as a process and as a tool for avoiding executive error is appropriate here. Descriptions abound of CEOs who make their decisions too quickly, who shoot from the hip. There are, of course, several problems with this approach, including the likelihood that executives can shoot themselves in the process. This failure appears to derive from the assumption that delay represents weakness and from an inability to make decisions effectively. The characteristics of the careful decision maker are not related necessarily to weakness, but rather to a more deliberate process. The precipitous decision often is made without adequate participation of appropriate individuals in the decision-making process; it can produce an end opposite to that intended. While some poor decisions are retrievable, many can and should be avoided initially.

The opposite occurs when decisions are not made at all, or are made so late as to be ineffective and impossible to implement. There are a number of mechanisms that administrators use to avoid decision making, particularly if the issue is difficult or delicate and if the decision itself can produce only problems. Some techniques to avoid decision making include amorphous/ambiguous problem definition, no timetable for decision trees, obscure communications, overly long adherence to prior decisions, and deliberate failure to delegate required authority. The emergence or presence of multitudinous committees that linger on for years are examples of that process.

An assumption is that all decisions require massive participation by hundreds of individuals, by extensive discussion of all the issues in great detail, and by the development of groups without specific charges that function more as discussion forums than as proper committees. This grows out of the lengthy list of potential interests in the decision (medical staff, employees, community), whose many members desire participation. Such approaches are defended on the ground that they allow extensive communication and maximum participation of all involved individuals; in truth, there is no way that everyone who wishes to be involved in major decisions can be, and it is clear as well that that is unnecessary.

There is a remarkable difference between attempting to develop a case that provides all the facts that could impinge on the decision, and one that produces a catalog of facts sufficient to make the decision, and it is the decisive administrators who seek the latter course. A middle ground is not necessarily appropriate. It is not unlikely that for careful and well-thought-out decisions, either approach can be part of the management style of a chief executive. However, to have either become the dominant style is a guarantee of eventual failure and a symptom of weakness. The overly quick and the too-slow decision makers both are weak. Their styles will lead, quickly or eventually, to consistent patterns of failure. Even providing such persons with good decision makers to buttress their indecisiveness will not preserve careers or forestall failure permanently. The only justification for either style is situational—its relationship to the timeliness of the decision making and the pace of change. It is redundant but possibly necessary to state that decisions made too late, no matter how accurate or correct, are useless and in fact are more demoralizing than no decisions at all. It is essential that a process of decision making be formulated, understood, and followed consistently.

The executive as leader must establish levels of decision making within an institution. Each level of supervision has a responsibility for as specific a set of decision-making opportunities as is possible. Clarity of that authority is essential if the process is to work. Obviously there may be amorphous areas, but the organization's philosophy ought to be that decisions be made by the individual most responsible for their outcome. Managers who seem reluctant to make decisions often argue that they are burdened with the responsibilities of office but do not have the authority to act. In fact, the reverse is true more often.

Some managers seem reluctant to exercise authority and instead pass the decision making to a higher level. Their development may be the key factor; that is, they may be unprepared to make decisions and reluctant to accept that responsibility. If that is true, then the senior-level executive must determine whether such managers are to remain with the institution in decisional positions.

For example, part of the solution may be in having them develop alternative decisions in a prescribed time frame that then can be discussed with the immediate superior for settling on a course of action. That may lead eventually to a pattern of successful decision making by such managers. In the absence of that decisive trait, it does provide an approach that uses individuals' talents, keeps them in the decision-making process, and does not put the full decisional burden on higher levels of supervision.

COMMITTEES AND THEIR FUNCTION

The identification of key decision makers in the institution is a necessary first step. To ensure that the decision-making process works, there should be a framework or apparatus that becomes the pattern for the approach used in the facility. The use of committees can be seen as avoidance of decision making, and often serves as an approach to procrastination.

A committee can have useful activities but its value may depend in significant part on how the group is structured. Every committee should be appointed with a specific charge: that is, a clear purpose and intended accomplishments. The members should be chosen carefully to cover issues that may be political in nature or that relate to the governance of the institution. They should be representative of individuals whose background, interest, and responsibilities relate to the committee's charge. The chair must be an individual who is skillful and experienced in this role.

If a committee is to develop a plan, the dimensions of that plan should be spelled out in the charge. If it is to make recommendations to a higher authority, that should be clear and the committee should understand that it is not coming to a final decision, but rather is developing a series of alternatives. It is important that the group be informed as to whether it is to reach its conclusion by a majority vote or by a consensus decision without a formal vote. A fact-finding committee can be useful as long as it is possible to define the dimensions of the issue under consideration and the material expected in its conclusive report.

Finally, the committee should operate under a sunset rule: a specific conclusion date should be part of its initial instructions. That may have the advantage of attracting individuals who lack patience with committees and who are unwilling to serve unless they understand that the activities will have a particular purpose and will terminate at a specific time.

Executives often are the subjects of a classification system that identifies them as autocratic, dictatorial, laissez-faire, or democratic leaders. These terms are useless in the sense that no individual practices the same style of management without some variations. In truth, senior management decision making cannot be a democratic process, and majority votes carry the danger of splitting a constituency. The institution's purposes and the executive's track record can be marred by decisions that are reached by narrow majorities. More acceptable to individuals is the opportunity to participate where appropriate in the process that leads to key decisions.

It is not simple to identify who should be involved in a particular decision. That underscores the need for a formal approach that goes beyond the kitchen cabinet method. While hospital executives who have developed trusting relationships with key individuals should use those informal channels to review ideas and to probe the depths of a problem, this process is likely to satisfy only part of the decision-making apparatus. It is the exceptional executive who will consult with dissidents—those generally opposed to the particular path being taken. A formal process that identifies all of the elements in the process will bring the dissidents to light but any attempt to force their inclusion will not necessarily be successful in each instance.

Inevitably, the hospital executives must make the major decisions—and alone. It must be understood in advance of the process that the CEOs will make the decision; however, if it is to be left to a group or committee, and that is stated at the outset, the executives are required to implement such decisions.

MEDICAL STAFF INVOLVEMENT

For too long a time, the relationship of the organized medical staff to the hospital administration has been assumed to be adversarial. Actually, there is more reason for management and medical staff to work closely together than there ever has been for being apart. The key issue now is to incorporate the medical staff into the management and decision-making process without sacrificing executive authority. Care must be taken to keep the physicians informed fully on any issues that will affect their livelihood and their ability to care for patients in the hospital. The effective use of medical board meetings is an essential part of executives' armamentarium.

Care must be taken to ensure that the CEOs' relationship with the medical board is not a subsidiary one, or one that sees them acting as the board's servant. Rather, the executives must be seen as the agents of the hospital's board of directors and firmly established as such by that body. The CEOs carry the fiduciary responsibility of the hospital board as its agent, as well as its responsibility for the care of patients admitted to the hospital or served in any of its modalities.

A regularized pattern of involving the president of the medical staff, the chief of staff, and/or the heads of the clinical departments is essential. The executive officer of the hospital should have developed a pattern of regular communications with such individuals and have formed a group that the CEO chairs to ensure its members' participation in the management of the institution. This is separate from the communication process in the sense that it is more than informational and stresses the role of the medical staff in its own governance and in the management of the hospital.

RELATIONS WITH THE BOARD

Too many hospital executives have found themselves relieved of their responsibilities by the board over issues that should not have gone that far. The hospital director must be more than an agent of the board in carrying out the trustees' general policy statements. The CEO must be a leader with the board while taking directions from it and must be seen as the individual who represents the entire hospital to its members. Obviously, the medical staff must have direct access to the board, but the chief executive must develop a relationship with that group that establishes the CEO as a decision maker for the panel. The CEO must carry the board's imprimatur. A useful technique is to avoid board members' participation in daily decision making but to include them in ad hoc and other relationships separate from board committees. This is a delicate process that makes the assumption that the executive who wishes to continue to succeed understands the informal use of the board in the administrative process.

PITFALLS AND FAILURES

It should be understood that making decisions that do not work out is not usually a cause for identifying such individuals as having failed in their executive performance. In an era characterized by rapid change, overcaution in the expectation that such behavior leads to impeccable decisions is a trap. So, too, is the knee-jerk response of joining the crowd in decision making, thus following current trends. What is important is that the decisions be made for good reason, and even in failure represent an opportunity worth having tried.

Without developing extensive rationales to anticipate possible failure, it is useful to indicate pitfalls when implementing new programs created as a result of management decision making. However, chief executives who evade making decisions that later do not work out are not making the decisions they ought to and not taking the reasonable risks associated with executive and organizational success. Dealing with the consequences of failure of decisions is important, and executives should use the nonsuccess in terms of building for future success or using the failure creatively as a learning device.

In 1948, Herbert Simon wrote of the fact/value dichotomy in decision making.[2] He pointed out that good decisions require understanding that facts alone do not constitute a base for decisions. Values carried and honored by individuals and organizations are equally important. It is important to remember that health care organizations are irrational in their structure, in their activities, and in their results—as is the entire health care environment. The attempt to apply a purely rational approach to decision making and to organization management reflects an unrealistic view of the context in which decisions are made in institutions. The elements that comprise executive leadership include the capacity to apply reason in an unreasonable situation and to inculcate the learned values that experience brings. Executives should be aware of the biases, cultural values, and experiential factors they bring to each of the decision-making and leadership situations in which they interact.[3]

In a simpler time, it was assumed that individuals developed an intuitional sense for the right and correct decision. It is likely that so-called intuition is the function of unconscious reasoning based on executives' history of experience and, it is hoped, a pattern of success. Most executives who achieve success find that reward occurs after substantial demonstrations of effective leadership. They must understand their personal qualities and their implication for leadership and decisiveness in an organization. Flexibility in the approaches, patterns, and degrees to which a rational decision matches the irrational world of the institution, and recognition that leadership of more than one style is appropriate and should be situational in nature, are to be blended into an executive method of operation that, while consistent, reflects the vagaries of the evolving environment.

Finally, a sense of proportion and ability to see the humor in organizations under stress is essential. This is left for last because it is probably most difficult to identify as a learned skill, but just as stress situations in other areas produce contextual humor, they must exist in the health care field as well. The familiar examples of humor exhibited by soldiers in danger, or the gallows humor characteristic of others in stress situations, have their parallel in the executive world and in health administration especially.

Incorporating that element into individual style in appropriate ways can support the leadership role and enhance the quality of the individual leading the institution. When all else is present in terms of the qualities of leadership discussed in this chapter, as well as in the other chapters in this book, it becomes the final winning grace.

NOTES

1. Alvin Toffler, *Future Shock* (New York: Random House, Inc., 1970).

2. Herbert A. Simon, *Administrative Behavior* (New York: The Macmillan Company, 1948).

3. William A. Cohan, *Top Executive Performance* (New York: John Wiley & Sons, Inc., 1985).

Effective Board-Administration Relationships

Newell E. France

11

Colonel Edward H. White, II, was the first astronaut to walk in space while on the Gemini IV flight in June 1965. In recognition of this unique accomplishment he was named to receive from the American Institute of Aeronautics and Astronautics the $500 Haley Award. When he was informed of this honor, Colonel White, rather than accept this honorarium, presented it to the Seabrook, Texas, United Methodist Church. It was understood that the money would be contributed toward the cost of building a youth center, which the community badly needed.

Contributions following Colonel White's were small but increased notably after the catastrophic fire on January 27, 1967, in the Apollo spacecraft in which he, Roger B. Chaffee, and Virgil E. Grissom were burned to death during a launch pad test in preparation for still another flight into space.

Although the fund had grown to the larger but still sadly inadequate figure of $80,000, it became the nucleus for the amount needed to complete the youth center, which was estimated to cost $350,000. Such a sum could not be raised in the small community of Seabrook, and outside funding sources had to be tapped. Naturally, the people of Texas were enlisted to help.

A small group of affluent senior citizens met with common purpose and enlisted the help of hundreds of young co-workers, including former astronaut Alan Shepard. The required amount was realized with a single fund-raising event.[1]

BEING YOUNGER IN YEARS

The leader of the Colonel White Memorial Youth Center project, a man senior in age, also chaired a hospital governing board. When asked by his (then) young administrator why these older persons took on the agony of

141

leading fund-raising projects that could be accomplished better by the younger co-workers, the administrator was referred pointedly to the essay "De Senectute" by Cicero, who observed,

> There is nothing then in the argument that old age is devoid of useful activity. To say that is like saying a steersman, sitting quietly in the stern and holding the tiller, contributes nothing to sailing a ship, for others climb the masts, run up and down the gangways, man the pumps. He may not be doing what younger men do, but what he does is better and more important. Large affairs are not performed by muscle, speed, nimbleness, but by reflection, character, judgment. In age these qualities are not diminished but augmented.[2]

Hospital executives who are younger in years than their board leadership must accept the fact that their capacity for good judgment, regardless of qualification, will always be subject to question and that selling recommending, rather than telling, will be an avenue to success. The elders of the board tend to receive well considered recommendations requiring action for their review and consideration.

When executives are younger than one or more of their board members and are dedicated to achieving a given result, the means to the end become paramount. Among these are the aspects of indirect leadership that include recognition that board and executives are not peers, that prior review and advice should be sought, and that a member of the board may be better situated to review, comment, and present an item for action.

Not to be forgotten is that young and old have their physical discomforts that affect their mental attitudes. The aging, however, seem to have what are termed "infirmities." A chairman of the board told his personal physician: "Give it to me straight, Doc. How many more golden years do I have still staring me in the face?"

When elder board members embrace the rationale of Cicero on serene old age, they may grow to resent the continuing requests for input, the energy drain caused by serious thinking, and the possibility that they, rather than the administrator, are doing the job. In the stress of the changing relationship, executives may develop an attitude toward the board that is perceived as condescension and in itself can lead to unexplained and unanticipated termination.

Dr. William Osler referred to the relative "uselessness" of men over 60, which a newspaper interpreted that all men over that age should be "chloroformed."[3] Needless to say, there was a markedly unfavorable reaction to that less than serious observation.

ACHIEVING THROUGH OTHERS

The author, promoted from within to executive director after 16 years of service, answered a telephone page in the Atlanta airport. The voice on the telephone said, "A new lifetime president has been elected who in his acceptance remarks dismissed the entire board. Do you plan to come back?" On return there was a waiting telephone message: "Call me when prepared to discuss your and the hospital's future."

The week-long agony that followed culminated in the preparation of a 35-page review of operations and a forward plan. The board president, who was an awesome man, then visited the author's office. He stood erect in the doorway, at first not choosing to enter. Upon accepting a welcoming hand-shake, he did enter and seated himself in a chair distant from the desk (where the comprehensive document lay). After a seemingly long moment of silence, he asked, "In your many thoughts over the past week, what have you determined to be the single, most important aspiration for the future?" The answer came, without hesitation, "To make you a great president." Again, after a long moment of silence, he rose from his chair, offered a handshake, and said, "We have nothing further to discuss."

The nine years that followed, ending with his death, are remembered less for achieving a worldwide reputation for the hospital than for being taught how to react to criticism with grace and to apply the varied dimensions of management science, always within the reach of possibility, to one's own and the hospital's professional life. In retrospect, the synergy that evolved came mostly from the need to respond to new and devoted leadership, his appreciation of the art of management, and the solid grounding of principles by which one was to work.

BOARD MAKEUP AND OPERATION

The candidates for service on the new board were qualified for election by (1) their commitment to attend not less than 10 of 12 regular meetings during the corporate year, (2) their history of recognized community and church involvement, and (3) their employment at the senior vice president level in corporate management. The 22 who were elected were male, female, black, and white. They were directly responsible for the entrepre-neurial, operations, or group services dimensions of their business; in addition, a church leader and an associate dean of a nonaffiliated university were elected. Not considered were representatives of fields with which the hospital would conduct business, with resultant compensation for services; namely, bankers, accountants, insurance agents, and physicians.

The mix that evolved included working professionals in the areas of operations administration, planning, marketing and public relations, human resources, law, finance, systems, construction, investment counseling, research, and education. The board's role in providing management oversight, consultation, monitoring of results, forward planning, community relations, education, research understanding, and self-education would be energized from within its membership.

A guiding principle applied by this president to the selection process, and to the question of physician membership in particular, was that to be intelligent is not necessarily to be knowledgeable; however, he said, those who are knowledgeable have the responsibility to teach when given the opportunity to do so and when an expectation of learning is imposed upon the student. That the members of the board were to become students of the clinical program with the medical staff serving as faculty proved to be a salutary and stimulating concept.

Physicians educated each board member about the clinical program. Senior management coordinated the interviewing, planning, and structuring of the informational effort. They provided a vehicle for integrated management by board, medical staff, and administration. Through discussion and questions the roles and relationships of each organizational component were defined and tacitly understood, rather than agreed upon. A singular step forward was the recognition of accountability by the medical staff members for what they said and did in matters other than the practice of medicine.

What administrative joy arose when the executive committee of the medical staff requested revenue and expense accounting by clinical service, a seminar on indirect expense allocation, and the budgeting prerogative for education and research—all based on awareness and new understanding that the bottom-line income is what pays for capital equipment and academic program development. Governing board members were pleased as they sensed that the medical staff was becoming responsive to institutional needs and that the thwarting of progress that stems from the quest for control was being replaced by movement toward commitment.

The emergence of a knowledgeable board and involved medical staff that no longer was peripheral to operations management precipitated among the administrative staff members a need for evaluating the effectiveness of their relationships to these groups, to one another, and to the varied management styles then existing. That they were to both give and receive cooperation became a management challenge. Group sessions and one-on-one conferences with the administrator and chief of the medical staff served to replace feelings of anxiety with self-confidence and fostered team building through collaborative management approaches to problem solving.

The board chairman contributed greatly to the issues discussed by articulating his expectations and management philosophy that, if accepted, would make for a successful outcome:

1. "Nobody speaks for the board but the board itself." Neither the board chairman, the chief executive officer, nor chief of staff may presume or assume board position in matters appropriate to or within the board's collective authority.
2. The board will not be inclined to receive negative recommendations, particularly as a recommendation may apply to a medical staff appointment. Board, medical staff, and administrative committee findings and recommendations will be received at board level for review and consideration but without obligation to act.
3. Individual members of the administrative staff serve at the pleasure of the board.
4. The prioritized essentials to operating a hospital are: Nursing Service, Food Service, Building Maintenance, and Finance. Additionally, positive medical staff administration relations are important (considering that governing boards seldom dismiss the medical staff).
5. The collective image of the board, medical staff, and administration to the hospitals' constituencies is important, the most significant constituency being the work force.
6. The essentials of leadership reside in positive human interaction, communicative skills, and the desire of two or more people to please each other.
7. Listen and hear, and if you have two eyes and a mouth, keep the obvious one shut.
8. One can do most anything, good and bad, when someone else is to get the credit.
9. The most damaging negatives, real or perceived, are any single display of incompetence, any disintegrative motive or comment, manipulation, and positioning that is politically influenced.
10. Criticism constructively intended is a valid aspect of teaching; when well received it is a contribution to learning.
11. Although the primary mission of the hospital is patient care, there is also primary responsibility to affiliated agencies with which there is mutual dependency or contractual obligation.

12. Motivation without enthusiasm, positive or negative, is a zero line in productivity measurement.
13. Envy to some degree exists within board members for those who work full time in the hospital.[4]

EFFECTIVE RELATIONSHIPS

It is apparent that interpersonal skills are paramount in developing effective relationships between the administrator and the board and medical staff. Traditionally, governing boards have sought to employ an administrator with a record of good medical staff relations, the hidden agenda being that if this is true there will be effective relationships with the board and employees.

The interpersonal skills required to relate effectively to nonsubordinates (the board and medical staff) and to subordinates (the employees) are varied in kind and application and are intended to achieve cooperation. At board level, the CEO's intent is to be perceived as credible through demonstrated proficiency in obtaining approval for plan or program implementation. The most important traits of the administrator vary also in perception among the three organizational dimensions, honesty and trust being foremost to the employees, responsiveness to the medical staff, and competence to the board.

Competency, in the judgment of the board, is less dependent upon maintaining good relations with the medical staff than on demonstrated ability in strategic and financial planning and marketing skills. The administrator who is relating to board members at committee or board level must keep in mind the priorities of interest and be able to respond to questions with facts and reasonably well-grounded predictions that are not based solely on conjecture. The executive must be well prepared, appropriately informed, enthusiastic, and committed to the institution and board.

COMPUTERIZATION ARRIVES

A relatively new element that is available to modern managers is the data bank. Thousands of bits of information can be gathered supporting or justifying an adjustment to policy, implementing a change, launching a program, conserving a cost, or enhancing a revenue opportunity. The author recalls providing each member of the board with a one-inch-thick printout as documented support for altering overtime and on-call pay. Following board approval, the chairman was asked for his reaction to the presentation; he responded in two words, "instantly forgettable." In his opinion time, money, and imagination were lost, the only thing not documented being common sense. Perhaps the secret to effective board relationships is experience in relating to authority, applied psychology, and an abundance of common sense that does not get lost in the shadow of information systems technology.

Unlike physician/administrator relationships, the executive does not meet with the board to defend fiscal viability or harmonize multiple authorities. Rather, the CEO serves as a resource for accurate decision making, long-range planning, marketing strategy development, the determination of space and funding needs, human resource management, and the identification of corporate objectives.

The administrator also shares responsibility with the governing board for its decisions and actions. While there is no question that the authority over the hospital's operation is indisputably under the jurisdiction of the governing board, it must be remembered that, more often than not, board "thinking" originates with the administrator. To be effective in relations with a board committee, the administrator should assume a position, if possible, as a member who is working with rather than for the committee. The executive will want to be effective not only in these relationships but also in bringing the committee's charge to a conclusion. More likely than not, the complexity of problems to be assessed and solved at board level require the inclusion of two or more administrative team members whose relationship is cohesive and collaborative. The opportunity to provide physician representation should not be overlooked, particularly if discussions pertain to long-range planning, corporate goals, or competitive intensity.

The economic realities of the future of hospitals dictate that considerable managerial ability will be required and that effective working relationships among administrators, physicians, and qualified board members will be essential to success. The board chair can be most helpful in providing a climate conducive to cooperative interaction, as can the administrator by shaping attitudes toward this end for associates and the medical staff.

The cornerstone of health care has always been people. The challenge for those who have patient care responsibility is to deliver it well. Effective relationships at all levels of the organization are necessary if patient care—the ultimate mission of the institution—is to be carried out.

BOARD-ADMINISTRATION RELATIONS

The institution's governing board consists of a group of individuals with whom the service of a public good has been entrusted. The board takes responsibility for governance, sees that the organization meets its obligations, establishes overall policies, monitors the implementation of its guidelines, and represents the community. Administrators dramatically increase their success potential if they have a harmonious, trustful, respectful relationship with the board. This does not mean the elimination of conflict but rather its successful management.

The board chair and the administrator must build a firm trust relationship. They should be able to level with each other and discuss honestly and candidly the issues before their organization. They must be in agreement as to how the board and administrative staff are to work together. They should agree on recommendations to the board or, if they differ, on how to present an issue with opposing views for board resolution.

Administrative staff members should keep in mind that the language of business and business people is figures; if this language requirement is satisfied, board members can better relate to the program.

Board members bring to the board-administration relationship:

- expertise in a variety of professional and technical areas that the organization otherwise would pay for
- influence to attract financial, human, and public relations resources
- an objective point of view of operations and the capacity for critical review
- knowledge of various facts about the community
- ability to effect change in the organization
- collective wisdom
- continuity of policy and program.

The administrative staff brings to the board-administration relationship:

- professional expertise in administrative functions
- basic knowledge of the organization
- ability to coordinate board activities and support, and to identify problems before the board members do
- public recognition and appreciation of board services.

The governing board members can reasonably expect of the administrative staff:

- attention to details of meetings and conferences
- judicious use of time
- complete, concise, and accurate information

- candor in individual and organizational relationships
- prompt return of calls and response to requests for information
- meeting of agreed-upon deadlines, with notification if deadlines cannot be met
- adequate preparation for meetings in which the board members play a leadership role.

The administrative staff can reasonably expect of board members:

- easy access by phone or visitation
- fulfillment of commitments within agreed-upon deadlines
- leadership, initiation rather than response, knowledge of the organization, and ability
- sensitivity to organizational problems
- support in controversial situations
- candid performance appraisals and assistance in performance
- loyalty and confidentiality.

NOTES

1. Leopold L. Meyer, *The Days of My Years* (Houston: Universal Printers, 1975), p. 123.

2. Marcus Tullius Cicero, *De Senectute.* Vol. XX. Translated by William Armistead Falconer. Cambridge, Mass.: Harvard University Press, 1971.

3. Harvey Cushing, *The Life of Sir William Osler,* vol. 1, chap. 24 (Oxford: Clarendon Press, 1925).

4. The Right Reverend J. Milton Richardson, bishop of the Episcopal Diocese of Texas, 1965–1980; president, Board of Directors, St. Luke's Episcopal Hospital, Houston, Texas, 1974–1980.

Qualities for Career Success

Pat N. Groner

12

The great historian Will Durant authored this statement in his *Story of Civilization:*

> When Demosthenes concluded his speech, they said: "How well he spoke." When Caesar ended his remarks, they cried: "Let us march!"[1]

That quotation is one of the best illustrations of the quality called leadership. In today's world the concept has been altered a little and some refer to it as "career success" for executives. But whatever the illustration, the point is this: In today's business and professional world there are some constants and some variables that measure career results of everyone.

How far they move up the ladder of success and how effectively their organization performs is directly related to several traits they either possess or master. Some of these success factors have changed little over the course of time. Others are in flux and are given greater prominence today in the leadership success profile. This chapter identifies these factors and provides illustrations and some pros and cons as they relate to modern health care institutions.

SURVEY OF THE SUCCESSFUL

As a preface, a word about the method of inquiry used. Two avenues were pursued: one was to review, with a few contemporaries, the career profiles of a number of our associates, past and present whose careers are models of success. The illustrations involving them, both current (in 1985) and from the fairly recent past, demonstrate the stability of some factors and the transient quality of others.

The second was to broaden that base, 26 men who are considered among the most successful in the field of health care delivery were contacted (see Table 12-1). These were 1985 members of the Hospital Research & Development Institute (HRDI)—men whose records range from unqualified achievement in their respective institutions to the principal chairs and trusteeships of the American Hospital Association and/or the American College of Healthcare Executives.

That exercise began in a rather primitive form. Each man was simply asked to list the elements he felt contributed to the character and performance of the successful person in this field, then to prioritize the listing. A further statistical analysis documented which factors, in their assessment, contributed to their own success in today's management environment. For purposes here, these were grouped into 17 qualities of leadership success.

"Qualities for Career Success," as a chapter title, carries the assumption that certain principles are universal (which in turn supports the assumption that a top-flight person could succeed in most management arenas). However, there are events of recent vintage that challenge this assumption.

Beginning with the early 1970s, when the United States found itself in a new era of competition from abroad, many major American businesses went through trying times, not unlike those facing hospitals in the 1980s. Looking back to that period, it is apparent that suddenly this country was outpriced, outsold, and generally outperformed in a variety of manufacturing fields ranging from steel and automobiles to textiles and machine tools.

For a decade *The Wall Street Journal* and a host of writers bemoaned the loss of national leadership in fields this nation had long dominated. Fingers were pointed in many directions. America's work force had become slack and less productive. Investment in up-to-date factories and equipment had lagged. Other countries' low-priced labor was giving them decided advantages and their governments were subsidizing production. Others claimed that this was a natural evolution from a manufacturing to a service economy.

Only when the national balance of payments continued to skew and budget deficits reached alarming levels did the country as a whole take a hard look at what was happening. Massive unemployment was developing as long-time industries lost their markets—domestic and foreign. A new national policy was required, and the country began to recognize that the core of the problem lay in the fact that many parts of the economy were being outled. Businesses that had thrived under leadership that might be termed "old fashioned Bull of the Woods entrepreneurship" were deteriorating. Many enterprises developed an obsession with costs, yet they did little to move their stagnant processes and management into the arena of modern requirements.

Table 12-1 Qualities for Career Success

	Basic Replies/Points	(5) Replies/Points	(4) Replies/Points	(3) Replies/Points	(2) Replies/Points	(1) Replies/Points	Total Listings	Total Points	Average of Total Points	Average of Listed Points
Ability to Communicate/Speak	16/160		2/8		3/6	2/2	23[2]* =	176[4]	6.77[4]	7.65[5]
Appearance/Poise	1/10				1/2	3/3	5[14] =	15[16]	0.60[16]	3.00[17]
Appreciation/Sensitivity	2/20			1/3	1/2	3/3	7[12] =	28[14]	1.08[14]	4.00[12]
Attitude/Motivation	10/100	7/35	1/4	4/12		1/1	23[2] =	152[5]	5.85[5]	6.61[6]
Community Leadership			1/4	1/3			2[17] =	7[17]	0.27[17]	3.50[16]
Decision Making/Decisiveness	19/190	5/25	1/4		1/2		26[1] =	221[1]	8.50[1]	8.50[3]
Drive/Hard Work	7/70	3/15	2/8	4/12	3/6	3/3	22[6] =	114[7]	4.38[7]	5.18[10]
Enthusiasm	2/20		4/16	2/6	3/6	3/3	14[11] =	51[11]	3.64[9]	3.64[15]
Ingenuity/Innovation	5/50	3/15	7/28	4/12	2/4	2/2	23[2] =	111[8]	4.27[8]	4.83[11]
Integrity	19/190	2/10		1/3			22[6] =	203[3]	7.71[3]	9.23[2]
Knowledge/Field	5/50	2/10	3/12	3/9	2/4	1/1	16[10] =	86[10]	3.31[11]	5.38[8]
Knowledge/Institution	2/20	1/5	2/8				5[14] =	33[12]	1.27[12]	3.85[13]
Leadership	22/220					1/1	23[2] =	221[1]	8.50[1]	9.61[1]
Loyalty	1/10		2/8	1/3	2/2		6[13] =	23[15]	0.88[15]	3.83[14]
Personal Consistency	3/30			1/3			4[16] =	33[12]	1.27[12]	8.25[4]
Sense of Accountability	7/70			3/9	7/14	1/1	18[9] =	94[9]	3.62[10]	5.22[9]
Vision/Broad Perspective	9/90	4/20	1/4	1/3	3/6	3/3	21[8] =	126[6]	4.85[6]	6.00[7]

*Each respondent listed five basic qualities, each of which was graded as 5. Thus, 130 basic qualities on 26 replies results in 5 listed qualities each.

Example: 23[2] = (#listings)[(ranking)]

LEADERSHIP

There were, and are, some notable exceptions. One is Lee Iacocca, the Ford-turned-Chrysler executive who succeeded in salvaging a motor car company whose prospects were dim. Iacocca's exploits are well-documented in his best selling book, hence are not rechronicled here.[2] However, it is a critical point in this thesis to note that what he did was to *lead*.

He stepped into a management vacuum, quickly identified the corporate problems, then generated a new mission and strategies. He did what few leaders do today—he recognized that true leadership requires a combination of many factors in a prioritized approach, and he used virtually all of them. He reestablished corporate credibility, reengineered financial stability, motivated his people, made hard decisions, applied a strong personal knowledge of the company, then used good old American hard work to drive his corporation back to where customers, financiers, and government believed in it.

Iacocca's example is fresh in everyone's mind. But consider another—in hospitals—that may be growing a bit dim now but should not be: Ray Brown. To many, Brown will always be the man whose vision and imagination first directed the American hospital from being a cottage industry to what it had to become, a dynamic part of big business, structured on the model followed by virtually every other major form of enterprise. During a career that was tragically cut short by his premature death, he helped introduce a professional quality to hospital administration. He helped establish health care graduate-level programs at several universities and was a dynamic force that translated the hospital chief executive's role from an old-fashioned superintendent to that of a modern-day corporate officer. That was no easy task. Yet he did it with a leadership style and force of character that incorporated the qualities described herein.

Perhaps the greatest factor in his arsenal was his ability to interpret the big picture and to see it for what it could be rather than what it was. He was persistent, a salesman for his concept, a man able to communicate, a visionary who saw what health care must become. Before the 1960s Ray Brown predicted the advent of a service economy and the expansion in health care that emerged. He did not head the nation's largest hospital system or make a million dollars a year for his efforts. But he applied sound principles of management at every turn, became an ideal to his peers, and kept flowing a constant stream of ideas that many could use practically to improve the system.

A similar formula can be applied to John Alexander McMahon, retired president of the American Hospital Association. He had one of the most difficult assignments possible, in part because it is the type of position that invites second-guessing and Monday morning quarterbacking. Consider the times. Alex McMahon directed the AHA through its most difficult period. He helped engineer change at a time when the dynamics of change were roaring out of control. If he had done nothing more than hold the many pieces of the organization together, it would have been a masterful accomplishment. He painstakingly sorted out countless elements, and somehow the nonsystem survived, did not become government-owned or -controlled, and, despite the ravages of inflation, continued on the path that Brown had foreseen. Hospitals have emerged into a format akin to the great commercial enterprises that have molded the American economy, thanks in no small part to McMahon, who contributed so much in maintaining a positive environment.

In looking at the element of leadership taken on its own, what has the country and the profession learned in these 10 to 15 years? Perhaps the greatest single lesson has been that success comes not from caution but from the proper balance of force, imagination, and a willingness to do the unusual. Iacocca did things others would not attempt. Brown was a dreamer and a driver. McMahon helped the industry survive because he combined the many talents that kept a system energized.

Perhaps this can best be summarized by citing an observation by one who will remain nameless here for obvious reasons. Paraphrased, his observation went like this: The American business scene began to suffer in the seventies because lawyers and accountants began to dominate the executive suites. Of course, those professions are essential to the success and stability of any enterprise. But, while there are many exceptions, professionals in those callings tend to be supercautious. That is the nature of their training. They are prone to emphasize what cannot be done. They are overly sensitive to routine and details when the great need is for innovation—the new and visionary. When leaders began to recognize this failing and to correct it, the American business scene entered a period of positive correction.

The same has surely been true of the hospital scene. Leaders who concentrated on operational details have been left behind in the era of restructuring and market positioning. What Iacocca did with boldness and imagination could never have been achieved by his cost accountant. The survey among the Hospital Research & Development Institute members (Table 12-1) placed leadership at the top of its priorities for career success.

It may be helpful to present the other factors that this survey identified and that are covered in examples to follow. Following leadership, they are listed alphabetically:

- ability to communicate and speak
- appearance and poise

- appreciation and sensitivity
- attitude and motivation
- community leadership
- decision making and decisiveness
- drive and hard work
- enthusiasm
- ingenuity/innovation
- integrity
- knowledge of the executive's field
- knowledge of the executive's own institution
- loyalty
- personal consistency
- sense of accountability
- vision and the broad perspective.

Some of these obviously are a combination of qualities but, taken as a whole, they constitute what these successful men believe are the elements that have contributed most to their career advancements.

Each of the remaining 16 qualities, as they were collectively prioritized in the survey, are explored next.

DECISION MAKING AND DECISIVENESS

Perhaps the most obvious part of successful executives' portfolios is the ability to make decisions. There are examples by the score of people who did, or did not, have this quality. The adage, "Do something, even if it's wrong!" suggests that many an organization is laced with those who find decisiveness difficult. Yet, in these times, hospital executives are forced into this process far more than in the past.

Not too many years ago, decisions in health administration only occasionally were large or complex by comparison with other industries. But with the coming of multisystems, joint ventures, high finance, and competition, this demand has changed. It once was possible to speak jokingly of the hospital where one executive could initiate a new service while another was trying to call a committee meeting. Not any more.

Today's hospital executives, to enjoy long-term success, must combine the aggressiveness of a Ted Turner and the decisiveness of a Margaret Thatcher with judgments that make their decisions effective. This demands the harnessing of information resources and the development of communication skills of subordinates.

Twenty-five and 30 years ago there were few or no assistants, no vice presidents, few people with whom the CEO could brainstorm. Like Harry Truman, the buck stopped with the CEO and, in retrospect, that was superb training. The CEO had to learn to make effective decisions and to be decisive. The staff and the hospital had no time to wait for the CEO to spend days analyzing and meditating on a decision.

Now the difficult decisions have become more complex, and they come more often. The up-and-coming young executive must learn that this is a cardinal part of the role. Decisions by consensus are always slow and frequently wrong. When executives move to the top, they command the decision spotlight—for better or for worse.

INTEGRITY

In a similar HRDI survey in the early 1960s, integrity was number one though now rated number three. Several comments from respondents paraphrased as follows demonstrate its essentiality:

> Today's hospital executives move far beyond their institutional walls. They have become figures moving in high finance, in national circles with others in their own allied profession, among many with whom their institutions may develop joint ventures. their word must be their bond—every action, every policy they support must bear the weight of law. In their approach to life as well as work, they must be persons others learn to trust instinctively.

A new concept in American business? No. The nation moved away from caveat emptor almost a century ago when the founder of Sears, Roebuck proved to customers that they could get quality merchandise with an honest guarantee by using catalog mail services, and people like J. C. Penney established standards for quality and trust by which they lived.

In the field of health care, there are many examples of integrity, yet one stands out so distinctively that it helps illustrate what the survey respondents meant.

More than a quarter of a century ago, two men founded a small company that entered the home and office cleaning business in Chicago. Through a fortunate happenstance, they were invited by a then young administrator to demonstrate their services to the Lutheran General Hospital in Park Ridge, Ill. It was then that Marion Wade and Kenneth Hansen established Service-MASTER and began one of the outstanding success stories in the health care field. As of this writing, Wade is gone and Hansen is semiretired, but their successors, Kenneth Wessner and William Pollard, have sustained an atmosphere of integrity that is seldom equaled in American business.

The corporate name, ServiceMASTER, was conceived to illustrate the religious faith of the founders and their successors. The business practices fostered under that banner are everything that might be expected in such circumstances. They are the kind of people who believe in the baker's dozen, the 18-ounce pound, the second mile. People who deal with them need not question their ethics nor fear that they will be short-changed. The firm's practices carry through to their employees, of course.

No wonder that the firm now serves one out of every four hospitals in the United States. It does not advertise much. Word of mouth, personal testimonies, and success by example are its hallmarks. It is the kind of successful personal and corporate image that testifies that peoples' words, indeed, are their bond. Successful hospital leaders, like growing numbers in other forms of enterprise, see their philosophy as the wave of tomorrow.

ABILITY TO COMMUNICATE AND SPEAK

This quality is the fourth most important success trait noted in the survey. Yet, in fact, all 17 are among the "most important" inasmuch as a single point of weakness impairs management and leadership effectiveness. There was a man, unexcelled in management ability, an innovator par excellence, whose outstanding leadership talents were denied to the national scene because of his inability to communicate to audiences and his fear of public speaking. At a hospital meeting four decades ago, this man's extreme frustration became apparent when, because of this inability and fear, a persuasive adversary of very modest ability carried the day on a critical issue.

In a companion part to the survey, the HRDI members were asked to list five areas in which they would improve "if you could do it over." The ability to communicate and speak led the list. This failing has been around forever. But it cannot exist in the life of successful executives. They must be able to communicate under just about any circumstance. Communication implies as much to one-on-one conversations about serious subjects as to a prepared address or written statement. Communication is logic in action. It also is a factor of time, and heaven knows how much of that executives waste because persons they deal with cannot compress ideas into short, meaningful statements.

A friend authored a management text that contains a brief section on this subject. His suggestions included having the members of the executive group of an organization work together to improve each others' communications performances. He urged organizations to discuss the need openly and to recognize that they can help one another. He wrote:

> You do not have to send the erring executive back to the college campus to help him. Simple exercises that require people to study their own writings and to edit and compress them into a short, terse, effective style can perform minor miracles for some.[3]

Few of us will achieve the abilities of a Franklin Roosevelt, Winston Churchill, Ronald Reagan, or Thomas Paine . . . but we can improve. It is never too late to become an acceptable speaker or a writer of competence. Often, the first step is for individuals to be honest with themselves, recognizing that they really could stand improvement.

ATTITUDE AND MOTIVATION

To many executives, having things operate with business-as-usual smoothness is all that they could ask. But do successful executives seeking the best from their careers accept this? Winners seldom are produced without the force that made them want to be the best. The most obvious illustrations of this have come from the fields of sports and military science. But there are good examples from the field of commerce, too.

For example, in the late 1960s United Airlines was in trouble. Service had become slow and sloppy, customers found the attitudes of some employees nonchalant and even surly at times. Then the company changed presidents. The new man, Edward E. Carlson, did not come on board with memos and whips. Instead, he bought himself several suits that traveled well, ordered some yellow pads, and began the long, long route around the airline's stations. Day by day, often with little advance notice, the new president dropped in to hold informal chats with staff groups. He did not make much of a speech. He did let people know that he wanted to hear about their problems and to accept suggestions they might have. People responded cautiously. After all, he was a new boy on the block and they did not know what to expect.

With his initial list of suggestions in hand, Carlson returned to his office and began initiating changes. Most of these were small, but they illustrated that he meant what he said in wanting things to improve. Overall, only a modest percent of the suggestions warranted implementation. Then he got a new supply of tablets and repeated the travel exercise.

The second time around the new president was a more familiar figure. His questions had a little more bite and, in addition to gathering data from on the scene, he began offering a few suggestions of his own—ideas that quietly inspired some people to begin doing a little more in housekeeping, a lot more in being cordial to customers.

Carlson's campaign for improvement did not bring dramatic changes overnight, but in a short time the spirit within that airline had turned 180 degrees. With a quiet I'll-lead-if-you'll-follow spirit and with down-to-earth communications, Carlson gained respect and gave respect back to his people.

In the world of sports, the examples of motivation are legion. A friend, Bob Richards (the two-time Olympics champion and spokesman for Wheaties), says that, in addition to working hard for 10,000 hours at a sports discipline, great athletes must have someone who leads them on, carries them over those troughs of despair that are bound to come when the pain of practice or the agony of defeat is present. Vince Lombardi became a football legend because his coaching methods made average players believe they were indeed champions—better than their competition. Billy Martin could come back to the Yankees, time after time, and somehow spark them to start winning again after another manager leading the same talent had failed.

And on and on and on . . . through the sagas of Bear Bryant, Casey Stengel, and Joe McCarthy.

The same need is present in the hospitals of today.

Thomas J. Peters and Nancy Austin, in their book *A Passion for Excellence,* coined the acronym MBWA—Management by Walking Around.[4] Their point is simply this: too many modern-day executives have become chairbound. They cannot find time to break out of their offices to meet and talk with people, to find out how they are doing, or to help consider programs that will inject the little extra spark needed from time to time.

Baptist Hospital, Pensacola, Fla. (of which the author is president emeritus), has had many programs of this kind. In the 1970s, one was called POP (Pride of Performance); a more recent program was called Caring and placed new emphasis on the need for employees at every level to truly care about performance and the welfare of patients. In the 1960s a productivity incentive plan was developed that enabled employees to share the financial rewards of cost containment in the era before Medicare and diagnosis related groups (DRGs).

All of these plans were successful and illustrate the point. Motivation programs need not be supersophisticated, expensive, or permanent, but they are necessary. It has been proved beyond a doubt that employees need periodic encouragement, to be reminded that superior performance requires something extra. It is the business version of the locker room pep talk.

Executives who do not recognize this and participate in it shortchange their organizations and themselves. They may be persons who can get in game-ready mental condition for every workday simply by staring in the mirror. Most people are not like that. They have ups and downs.

Recognizing this and utilizing personal as well as staff motivational efforts is a must. Back in the dark days of the Depression, men stood in lines for hours to find a job so they could earn a day's wages; their motivation was that they needed to eat. Today's life style is different. Having a job does not necessarily certify that employees will give their all for 60 minutes of every hour. They need help.

VISION AND THE BROAD PERSPECTIVE

The world is full of success stories of the wisdom of people who anticipated great discoveries or market trends. They exist in the field of health care, too, but, if the truth be known, most health care executives have been followers, not innovators. Like those in other professions, they flock to seminars and conventions and spend countless hours scanning literature hoping to find a jewel that will add to their institution's bag of competitive tricks or to their own professional polish. There is nothing wrong with that. In fact, having a truly broad perspective of their field of work is critical to success for all executives. However, it is not enough to know what is going on today; tomorrow counts even more. Being knowledgeable about trends, the successes of others, the ideas of a genius in some far-away place helps guide planning.

One example is that hospitals were literally caught flat-footed by the computer age. There are numerous horror stories to illustrate this. Good executives lost their jobs and their reputations because they either moved too quickly or not quickly enough. This occurred because, when computers became a business reality, most hospital staffs were small. The chief executive often was too old to become personally interested and frequently had no one of sufficient ability to whom to delegate the responsibility. As a result, computer science in hospitals grew like Topsy, often with results that were career shaking.

What will be the next career-shaking innovation? Executives can rest assured there will be many. How will they anticipate the next wave? They need to have the qualities of vision and a broad perspective.

A friend tells a story about the founder of the Armstrong Cork Company. Thomas Armstrong, a bank teller, dreamed of owning his own business and by chance chose corks. (In those days all bottles were closed with hand-cut corks that were carved from pieces of cork-oak bark by men using murderously dangerous knives.) Armstrong started his little shop, maintaining his bank position and fulfilling the management needs of the business on evenings and weekends. Things went well until one day the entrepreneur called upon a customer who dug into a drawer and produced a sack of corks as alike as peas in a pod. "Why," Armstrong said, "these look as though they were made on a machine." "And they were," replied the customer. "In Philadelphia a man has produced a new lathe that does this beautiful job. I'm sorry, but I shan't be wanting your corks any longer."

That night, discussing the incident with his wife, Armstrong made this philosophical observation:

> Up until today I thought that management meant sales, directing the work force, and keeping the accounts. Today I learned that there is a factor which surmounts all of these. That is looking ahead . . . and knowing what is going to take place that might affect our business.[5]

This is said to be a true story. Certainly the story line is every bit as realistic for hospital leaders today. No executives can move to the top and remain there without the broad perspective. How they get it is something they must determine for themselves individually. The important point is to be alert to the need and then never to lose sight of the requirement.

DRIVE AND HARD WORK

How much does hard work and plain old drive count in the ultimate success of health care executives? They are important, but hardly at the top of the priorities list, according to the respondents to the HRDI survey. Not that these 26 men do not work hard. They do. Some are workaholics. Yet others live by the "work smarter" philosophy and do very well. Of course, there are scores of conflicting opinions on this, some claiming that delegation is the key to permitting executives to use their mental powers more fully, while others say that from time immemorial hard work has led to success.

A very successful hospital executive of a generation ago had on the wall behind his desk a floor-to-ceiling drape that, when parted, revealed a sign stating, "If You Enjoy Hard Work, You'll Have a Helluva Good Time Here." A frequent expression of the author's over the years has been, Hard Work Builds Character. Even the effective delegator is a hard worker, though not appearing to be.

Two friends, each of whom could serve as the epitome of these differences in management philosophy, come to mind. One "dislikes Wednesday meetings because they cut into both weekends." The other finds equal enjoyment in being a seven-days-a-week traveler and workaholic. In terms of their accomplishments, there is not a dime's worth of difference between the two. Though he might deny it, the first friend is "working" most of his waking hours, even on the golf course. The author has come to the conclusion there is more similarity than difference in their philosophies; one is working while he is having fun, the other is having fun while he is working.

INGENUITY/INNOVATION

"Everything that can be invented has been invented." Charles H. Duell, director, U.S. Patent Office, 1899.

"Who the hell wants to hear actors talk?" Harry Warner, Warner Bros. Pictures, c. 1927.

"There's no likelihood man can ever tap the power of the atom." Robert Millikan, Nobel Prize in Physics, 1923.

"Heavier-than-air flying machines are impossible." Lord Kelvin, president, Royal Society, c. 1895.

These were four points in an advertisement by TRW, Inc., in *Forbes* magazine.[6] For every advancement in technology, science, or management, there have been hundreds of authorities on the particular subject who said it could not be done. Fortunately, accelerating inventions, technical advantages, and knowledge breakthroughs are reducing the ranks of those whose bywords have been "It can't be done" and "We've always done it that way." Nonetheless, it is easier to criticize than create and, unfortunately, the critical rather than the creative person frequently has the more visible credentials. Perhaps this is so because being learned in present-day knowledge tends to reduce individuals' ability to think in terms of new knowledge.

In the pre-Medicare sixties, Ray Brown inquired into the payment patterns of Blue Cross plans across the country. Comparing areas in which cost reimbursement was predominant with those in which Blue Cross paid hospital charges, he found that in the former, hospital expenses and charges to patients were rising higher and at a greater rate. With the coming of Medicare, Brown urged that a prospective price program for hospital payment be adopted.

Although he was perhaps the most knowledgeable generalist in hospital management, there were others in the country regarded as more knowledgeable health care economists. The latter were supported by politicians anxious for quick passage of Medicare legislation, and they prevailed. Thus, cost reimbursement became the predominant method for payment for hospital services. Precisely at that moment, hospitals moved from the last semblance of a traditional marketplace into a contrived health care environment. Billions of dollars in waste and the present trauma in hospital and medical costs and care stem from that tragic mistake.

It has been said that an innovator with a new idea "has a hard time explaining it to himself, let alone someone else." While innovation in and of itself ranks high in today's world, it probably is too much to expect this to be a predominant trait in chief executive officers. Nevertheless, a strong bias toward innovation is vital in the organizational world. There is no future in believing that something cannot be done. Top leaders must be ingenious problem solvers and kindred spirits to the less-disciplined innovators. Both are musts in the modern health care organization.

SENSE OF ACCOUNTABILITY

Who accepts the blame when something goes wrong?
Who takes the bows when things are going well?
Who establishes the rules that relate to accountability?

These are not easy questions, and in many organizations they go unanswered. Too often, the responses are finger pointing in bad times, accolades for the executive suite when things are coming up roses. This is not the way to ensure executive success, according to the survey participants.

During and before World War II, the top person in most community hospitals usually was termed superintendent, with responsibilities of a supervisor rather than of a management nature. While hospital history is replete with the names of men and women who were strong and effective chief executives, management accountability generally was more of a board concern. After all, the hospital then was not a business.

This is not true today, nor has it been for many years in effectively operated hospitals. The major community health care provider frequently is the largest employer and business in town. Its CEO is highly trained and is supported by a staff of skilled professional managers. The degree of accountability has been compounded in two dimensions: management evolution and institutional growth. Governing boards, while still ultimately responsible both legally and morally, must delegate greater responsibility and authority to chief executives and hold them accountable. Thus, CEOs must have a high sense of accountability that permeates every action.

In recent years polls and historians have ranked Harry Truman among the nation's great presidents. Truman had a strong sense of accountability. During the author's career there have been many promising young hospital executives whose only noticeable shortcoming was their lack of this quality, their reluctance to make the tough decisions. (In fact, this may be the major roadblock to success.) Invariably, their modus operandi was to place controversial issues on the agenda of the next meeting of the board of directors. These young men lacked that sense of accountability so necessary to top managers who must, by decisive and effective actions, gain the respect of all elements of the organization.

KNOWLEDGE OF THE FIELD

Aside from being part of a winning hospital team for more than 30 years, the author's greatest professional satisfaction has come from being associated with top professionals from other hospitals across the country. One such person is Donald C. Carner. In the 1950s, he provided the leadership in bringing together a group of young, successful, and creative administrators. Several friends were in the original group (which accounted for the author's association, beginning in 1957). The group's activities were simply exchanges of reports, mutual assistance on projects, questionnaires and surveys, and two brainstorming sessions each year.

The benefits gained are obvious, one of which was to help each member achieve a better knowledge of the field. In every meeting, members received kernels of wisdom and imaginative challenges from professionals such as Ray Brown; Frank Groner, President Emeritus, Baptist Memorial Hospital; Tol Terrell, past administrator, Shannon West Texas Memorial Hospital; and Ron Yaw, retired President Emeritus, Blodgett Memorial Medical Center; along with the leader Don Carner, publisher, *Health & Care Magazine*. Originating from this group was the Hospital Research & Development Institute (HRDI), which has had a major impact on health care delivery and which provided the impetus for two impressive advances in health care organization.

One was Multihospital Mutual Insurance, Ltd. The idea of an offshore mutual insurance company to address the then impending malpractice crisis was first brainstormed in 1974. A charter for such was obtained in Bermuda. On November 1, 1975, MMI, Bermuda, began operations. A year later a similar company was established in the Cayman Islands for medical staff members of MMI hospitals. Three years after that, at the invitation of Lloyd's of London Group, the MMI companies chartered an excess carrier in London. In 1983 the MMI group moved on shore with the acquisition of American Continental Insurance Company.

The MMI group has enjoyed great success as one of the so-called "bedpan mutuals." With a few others, it led the way to an innovative and effective means of addressing the midseventies crisis in malpractice coverage. MMI and similar companies continue today as perhaps the most effective insurance mechanism for health care providers. MMI has preserved a good market with providers, saved many millions of dollars, and created additional millions in equity.

At the outset, MMI leadership realized the importance of selecting good risks. By insuring hospitals and physicians through companion companies, jurisdictional squabbles were avoided. Operating costs have been about a third of those of the average stock company. Its knowledge of the field enabled MMI membership to make decisive moves in an untried arena and to enjoy exceptional success.

In 1973 HRDI financed a study by a leading consulting firm to determine the feasibility of creating a national nonprofit hospital company. The results were strongly positive, and such an organization was chartered in 1974. It failed. Part of its failure can be attributed to a lack of appreciation—or knowledge of the field—of what was then happening in health care delivery. A few years later a Phoenix-like organization, Voluntary Hospitals of America, arose from the ashes of the earlier company. VHA's success is well known and many of the adherents of this concept believe it to be the second-generation national hospital company.

ENTHUSIASM

Over the years, many executives have had the privilege to work closely with quite a few individuals who could be classified as fireballs. Their level of enthusiasm exceeded the norm severalfold. They practically bubbled in their actions and viewed each day as a new opportunity to do something. For some, this type of enthusiasm is contagious; for others, it provides only a so-so result.

Another type of enthusiasm is not so outwardly evident. That is the enthusiasm of people who like what they are doing, find it challenging, and the results achieved are recognized and appreciated. The first type is not a career essential, the second type is. It has been the author's observation, without exception, that the health care CEO who is successful on balance and over time maintains a lasting enthusiasm for the job. When enthusiasm is lost, it is time to quit.

Though tied for 12th place on the list of priorities in the HRDI survey, enthusiasm is an essential quality for career success.

PERSONAL CONSISTENCY

This does not require that a person be very steady and have a benign personality. Simply, it is a naturalness and a steady pattern of behavior.

Iacocca operates in the fast lane with its emotional ups and downs, but his behavior is consistent. Reliability is a companion term.

Anyone who watches TV sports becomes conversant with the term consistency. It means playing up to the potential day after day, game after game. The term performs well when the key players do their thing. The star who is up today and down tomorrow seldom leads the team to the championship.

The same holds true in health care management. Subordinates want to be able to "read" the work patterns of the boss. Executives whose style does not remain level in times of trouble, or who deviate from the norm when personal problems or outside influences interfere, are hard to follow. Consistency is something everyone appreciates in those with whom they sustain long-term relationships. Some executives with great potential fail to enjoy high-level careers because they do not recognize the demands for consistent performance. In today's business world, when executive perks can undermine performance, it is more important than ever to recognize this point.

KNOWLEDGE OF THE INSTITUTION

There are many theories about how much chief executives must know about their organization. For example, how much can the president of a multinational conglomerate know about the vast operations of the company worldwide?

Until the 1970s, hospitals were relatively small, self-contained units— islands unto themselves. Growth and diversification has changed all that and has added tremendously to the scope of operations that chief executives must comprehend.

Can they have a full-scale understanding any more? How important is a knowledge of the many integrated parts of the whole as compared with the essential principles of management?

These are questions that hardly concerned health care executives until recent years. Now they are in the forefront and forcing many persons to alter their traditional methods of operation. "The way we used to do it" no longer is applicable. If the question had been posed to the author a decade ago, he would have been forceful in support of the MBWA concept. People needed to know their chiefs, and the bosses needed to have a good understanding of total operations. While still desirable, such practices seem to be eroding.

One of the author's close friends, whose career has been nothing but success, believes that the health care executive has become an executive in the same sense as the person who runs an insurance or manufacturing company. There is no way he can be effective and still devote a large percentage of his time to being "totally knowledgeable" about what occurs in his institution. His goal now is to understand those items that count and to be sufficiently visible to present the proper management image.

Thus, defining the degree to which chief executives remain heavily involved and fully knowledgeable on parochial affairs is difficult. It is hoped that their peers will never divorce themselves totally from the nitty-gritty and be confined to their office suites.

Nonetheless, if they are to be accountable and if they have the proper staff to handle onsite chores, then perhaps the methods used by the one-man administrators should be things of the past. Great pleasure can be derived from being part of the action and, insofar as that is possible, it still can be useful. But in the larger institutions, this is anachronistic. Being true managers, getting results, being accountable, and meeting the obligations as they are now defined may have removed chief executives from the universal knowledge base and put them in positions where their effectiveness can do most for the institution.

APPRECIATION AND SENSITIVITY

Historically religious faiths in America have viewed hospitals as an important ministry. The author's father was a minister and educator whose strong ancillary interest in hospitals motivated his three sons and a host of young people to enter service in the health care field, recognizing that care, concern, appreciation, and sensitivity played as important a role in the patients' well-being as medical science. Other things being equal, an appreciation and sensitivity to the interest of others is unquestionably a career enhancement.

As peers view this factor today, there is a question about its importance in career success. How much will sensitivity count in creating a worthwhile organization? How will that factor be judged by trustees and others when they evaluate the executives and ultimately reward them? These few observations:

Appreciation and sensitivity are qualities that some people are born with in abundance but others must work diligently to cultivate. In the long run, their presence can have a large impact on the image of an organization, and certainly on successful staff development. Executives who go out of their way to make certain that career path planning is present and observed in the development of subordinates are doing what must be done to ensure the successful presence of many of the other factors mentioned. Their personal concern for patients must be a cardinal point in their understanding of what goes on in their institutions.

A hospital is not just a building or numbers on reports; it is a service provided by people for people. CEOs have to set an example, and how well they do so is going to have a marked effect upon how everyone, from the mail clerk to the vice president for nursing, addresses their duties. However, the consensus in the HRDI survey indicates that this factor is not close to the top of factors that successful executives will keep at the head of their own priority lists. Are these two elements necessary in a well-run hospital? Absolutely. Should these factors dominate executives' work and style? Probably not.

LOYALTY

For many, an early recollection of the word "loyal" probably occurred during their Boy Scout or Girl Scout years. Its part in Scout law usually leaves a lasting impression. In the survey results, it was interesting to note that loyalty had a high expression of interest for its relatively low ranking. The response of two HRDI members is significant: both said it should be classified as an element of integrity.

For those who read biographies and history, it is difficult to recall great leaders who did not have a strong sense of loyalty. It brings conflict, inasmuch as people with strong loyalties are sometimes faced with the decision of what is right versus being loyal to a friend. Blind loyalty is not virtue and, faced with such a problem, strong leaders usually have made the correct choice.

Also to be considered is institutional loyalty. Many outstanding executives, tempted by attractive offers of higher compensation at larger institutions, decline because of strong loyalty for the institutions they serve. H. Robert Cathcart, president of Pennsylvania Hospital in Philadelphia, the nation's first hospital, is the author's favorite example of institutional loyalty. A past chairman of the American Hospital Association and president or chairman of practically every organization or committee with which he has been associated, he has spurned offers over the years, opportunities with higher pay and fewer trials and tribulations.

His loyalty to Pennsylvania Hospital, its history and its traditions, is something to behold. This loyalty has paid rich dividends to that city's heritage in the culmination of the magnificent renovation program to which he has devoted 30 years. Cathcart has made the right decision, but so have many others who have chosen to accept new challenges. Years of observation provide the answer: individuals are happier and more successful in positions that offer the greatest potential for service. This principle should outweigh blind loyalty, and the HRDI survey respondents generally have applied the same judgment to their own decisions.

APPEARANCE AND POISE

When the returns were received from the initial mailing on the HRDI survey, it seemed logical to place the several attributes relating to appearance and poise together. In retrospect, based on the final tabulation, these are not necessarily similar qualities. Poise comes close to being an essential quality, appearance does not.

Newspaper and magazine ads would justify the conclusion that "clothes do make the man or woman." Much emphasis today is placed on personal appearance, from clothes to hairstyling to monogrammed shirts. Several consultant friends say it is company policy that they wear pinstriped or dark suits whenever they make a presentation. Some tend to be too suave, thus creating a not-too-positive first impression. A friend describing the qualities of another who had been the successful leader of a successful enterprise closed a series of compliments with this statement: ". . . and he walks into the offices of the CEOs of these billion-dollar companies in his double-knit plaid coat and trousers, and they love him."

Considering appearance alone, a reranking probably would place this quality in deep, last place. A good appearance is sort of a benign asset. A mode of dress that in itself attracts attention, one way or the other, is a liability. One response sums it up pretty well: "Look well, but do not go overboard."

Poise is something else. There are times when successful executives must sustain themselves under pressure, when they must react calmly to situations that are trying and unexpected. Poise is something individuals must create and develop since it does not appear to be a hereditary trait. Other things being equal, those who can maintain their "cool" and poise under pressure undoubtedly will carry the day.

COMMUNITY LEADERSHIP

This is an essential element, but was ranked last in the final tabulation. In a similar survey of HRDI members about 20 years ago, community service carried a high rating. This may be another sign of the times—a hospital of 20 years ago was always a "community" enterprise, which is not necessarily so today. Service on its board of trustees frequently was one of the highest callings for civic leaders. Naturally, it was important that hospital administrators reciprocate in service to the community.

In 1970 Baptist Hospital in Pensacola had its only postopening (1951) capital fund drive. It was, by far, the most successful effort of its nature in the city's history, with results far beyond the expectations of the board members. One of the reasons for success clearly was the community service provided over the years by so many persons associated with the hospital. Hospital leaders also had been the leaders in the United Fund and all other civic charitable groups. They had earned a lot of chips to call in.

In the growth of the health care industry, multisystem development, diversification, and other changes in the evolution toward bigness have diminished the philanthropic dollar and moved other priorities ahead of community leadership. Still, a 1981 article titled "Administrative Success: Key Ingredients" stated: "All of the leading executives said it [community involvement] was very important and essential." Quotes from top executives included the following:

"Community involvement is extremely important for any citizen, health executive or not."

"This involvement is more than the product of my own success."[7]

No doubt, the executives' locale has much to do with the importance of community leadership. Many of the HRDI executives are in major hospitals in large cities and others are CEOs of major nonprofit health care systems. In those instances, community leadership does not appear to be as important. For those in average-sized communities where the institutions are among the area's major enterprises, this quality assumes much more significance.

AUTRE TEMPS, AUTRE MOEURS

In summation, the survey on qualities for career success necessitated the use of examples to help readers remember the highlights. A survey in the sixties took a different form, but it was interesting to note that, with only 10 respondents, it produced a list of more than 70 qualities. No run-off election was held. In that survey, integrity was the only quality cited by all participants. The top ten qualities they selected were:

1. Integrity
2. Appreciation and Sensitivity
3. Tie $\left\{\begin{array}{l}\text{Community Leadership}\\\text{Drive and Hard Work}\\\text{Ingenuity and Innovation}\end{array}\right.$
6. Accountability
7. Tie $\left\{\begin{array}{l}\text{Attitude}\\\text{Ability to Communicate and Speak Well}\\\text{Decision Making and Decisiveness}\\\text{Knowledge of the Field}\end{array}\right.$

At the beginning of this chapter it was noted that many of the qualities for success had changed little over the years, while others are in flux and may be given greater prominence at one time than another. Considering that top health care executive officers of today bear only partial resemblance to their predecessors of the 1960s, perhaps the quality assessments were not too inconsistent. Differences that do exist are justified by the dramatic institutional changes and advances in organization and management knowledge during the intervening time.

It is hoped that this exercise will be beneficial to younger health care executives. Everyone recognizes that in today's environment, executives are required to make greater efforts and continuing commitment to a planned program of self-improvement if they are to succeed. If this exercise makes a contribution in that direction, then it will have been worthwhile.

NOTES

1. Will Durant, *Story of Civilization,* vol. 3 (New York: Simon & Schuster, Inc., 1944).

2. Lee Iacocca, *Iacocca* (New York: Bantam Books, Inc., 1985).

3. Jacob F. Horton, *Management Tier Systems* (Pensacola, Fla.: Pensacola Junior College Foundation, 1985).

4. Thomas J. Peters and Nancy Austin, *A Passion for Excellence* (New York: Random House, Inc., May 1985).

5. *This Is Armstrong.* Produced by Cameron Hawley and Columbia Pictures, 1949. Film.

6. TRW, Inc. advertisement, *Forbes,* November 18, 1985, 118.

7. Walter J. Wentz and Terence F. Moore, "Administrative Success: Key Ingredients," *Hospital and Health Services Administration* (Special II 1981): 85–93.

The Physician as a Manager

Bruce E. Spivey, M.D., and Lois M. Tow

13

In the past several decades physicians usually have held limited management roles, such as chairman of a clinical department or chief of staff, but in recent years their numbers among the ranks of professional managers is growing. Physician CEOs are a small group, but their impact is widening and physicians are seen in middle management with increasing frequency.

This emerging trend has to be highly threatening to most of the present senior management of medical centers. While physicians play a unique role as the central providers of health care services, they generally are perceived as emotional and inept managers. They have the potential to add a new dimension to health care management by combining their clinical training and experience with traditional management skills, but they often do it poorly.

Physician managers find themselves facing many challenges, not the least of which is their lack of formal training in management. Their clinical training does not prepare them to be professional managers of complex organizations. To be effective, their weaknesses must be overcome and their strengths developed so that the health care system can benefit from the unique and powerful contribution that well-trained physician managers can make.

THE EMERGING TREND

The 1980 Graduate Medical Education National Advisory Committee report predicting a physician surplus, and the subsequent fruition of that prediction, have fueled speculation that increasing numbers of physicians will move into management.[1] At the turn of this century (coincidentally in the midst of a prior physician glut) essentially all hospital CEOs were physicians. Once again physicians are moving into senior management and

177

chief executive officer (CEO) positions. This trend is predicted not only to continue but also to increase.

Interest in the topic has resulted in more studies. The American College of Hospital Administrators (ACHA) reported a 75 percent decline in physician CEOs from 1972 to 1982. However, from 1982 to 1983 they increased 27 percent to a total of 262 leading 3 percent of the nation's hospitals.[2] Physician administrators polled by the American Medical Association and Arthur Young & Company feel that they are part of a new direction that ultimately will bring more doctors into positions of responsibility in hospital management.[3] The empirical data documenting the trend are limited but the belief that it will continue is strong.

One indicator of this emerging trend is the development of professional organizations for physician managers. The Society of Medical Administrators, an elite group with few members but an influence disproportionate to its numbers, has been in existence since 1909. More recently, the American Academy of Medical Directors (AAMD) was formed in 1975 and by its tenth anniversary it had attained a membership of more than 1,500. The AAMD has spawned the American College of Physician Executives, which uses the traditional process of credentialing and examination to admit fellows.[4] Other such organizations are proliferating.

Physician managers' responsibilities vary widely. So far, most have been limited to overseeing medical staff affairs and contributing to the development of goals and objectives, policies and procedures, and new programs. Few physician "managers" are responsible for program management or budgetary control.[5] It is almost as if hospitals have decided that the best way to keep physician managers out of mischief is to keep them so busy planning and organizing that they will not ask why they do not control any resources.

At the opposite end of the spectrum are the 200 physician CEOs found in the ACHA study. This wide variation in extent of management responsibilities seems related to the qualifications of the job. Positions traditionally requiring MDs manage in only a very limited sense, without full management responsibility and authority. Obviously, physicians in management positions usually held by non-MDs must manage in the full sense of the word.

Most physician managers did not set out on a career path toward management. They find themselves drawn into management for a variety of reasons, including but not limited to:

- an opportunity to influence the direction of an organization and the challenge that entails;

- frustration at the status quo—the feeling of helplessness translates into the desire to effect change in the organization;
- by default—nobody else is willing to assume the responsibility, and it is better to manage than to be managed;
- to achieve specific goals—use of the managerial role to wield power for a given purpose or set of objectives;
- boredom with clinical practice; "burn-out" leading to the search for new areas of growth and competence.[6]

The turbulent health care environment is the strongest force pushing doctors into management. Physicians want to control the changes that are occurring in the health care system and are beginning to see that having their own kind in management is a way of achieving control. Recent medical school graduates are products of a changed environment in which the public has a greater health awareness and an expectation that traditional institutions should be responsive to their needs. These physicians, unlike their predecessors, will go into management purposefully in order to improve the health care delivery system. In addition, with the increasing surplus of physicians, many who move into management will do so because it looks more secure economically than struggling to keep a practice viable.[7]

Obviously, the involvement of physicians as professional managers in alternative delivery systems is increasing. It seems reasonable to expect that this site of entry into management may show the fastest growth in the near-term future. Regardless of the financial organization involved, however, the principles discussed here will apply.

Another push for physician managers is coming from hospital trustees. Mitchell Rabkin, M.D., president of Beth Israel Hospital, Boston, sees a renewed interest in physician CEOs because health care is at a turning point where cooperation among physicians, administration, and the board is critical.[8] The physician administrators surveyed by the AMA and Arthur Young concurred. They felt that their boards preferred to have a physician leading the organization.[9]

STRENGTHS AND WEAKNESSES

Physicians often are characterized as poor managers. As with most generalizations, the case is overstated. However, when the strengths and weaknesses that physicians bring to management roles are analyzed, the doctors are short on strengths.

Physicians' weaknesses in management should not be attributed to sloth or inability. Physicians' training and experience are different from that of professional managers. Comparing and contrasting clinical and managerial roles reveals the sources of some of the difficulties physicians face. The most fundamental reason why most of them are not good managers is that they are trained to react, but managers are trained to be proactive. Another difference is that the physicians are doers, while managers get work done through others.

Physician managers must reorient the way they work. Patient care physicians' rewards are often immediate and tangible while managers' rewards are delayed and vicarious. Physicians are the authorities who direct patient care, while managers must delegate authority in order to achieve the organization's goals.[10] Physicians do not delegate well. A nearly universal complaint is that they delegate responsibility without the concomitant authority.

Physician managers play a boundary-spanning role. Making the transition from one discipline to the other is not easy and requires an honest self-assessment of strengths and weaknesses.

Strengths

The physician managers' most obvious strength is their knowledge of and dedication to health care. They know firsthand what physicians think and do and how they play their games. Physicians spend a lot of time talking about "a better way" to do things in the health care system. Their ideas range from mundane hospital operations changes (e.g., convenient location of dictation system telephones) to far-reaching health care financing plans (e.g., formulas for equalizing the perceived procedural bias of the reimbursement system). Because of their greater access to physician colleagues, physician managers can harness those ideas and put them to work.

In today's health care environment, the concept of down-sizing has become popular. Yet overzealous or panicked managers may cut out too much flesh along with the fat. Physician managers' insight can help a hospital avoid cutting where it will hurt patient care.

For example, a medical center that had outpatient services scattered throughout many buildings provided a shuttle service for patients to and from the main parking lot. When a new outpatient services building was opened adjacent to the parking lot, the management team considered eliminating the shuttle service. Most of the center's outpatient visits now would occur in the new building just steps from the parking lot. However, a physician member of the team pointed out that the services whose patients were most likely to use the shuttle (geriatrics, physical therapy, and a clinic for the blind) were not moving into the new building. The shuttle service was retained.

While physician managers can be advocates for the doctors' viewpoint, they also can see through physician double talk. In addition, they are in a better position than the rest of the management team to challenge physicians when they are not being realistic. One physician CEO has said, "One of my greatest strengths is that I can smell doctor B.S.!" and, "When a doctor claims he is being the patient's advocate, sometimes he is really concerned about his own income, and I can call the question more easily than a nonphysician."[11]

Physician managers can make good use of the mystique attached to physicians. Even though public esteem for doctors has declined, people still assume that physicians put quality of care first. Therefore, the physician managers will be trusted to strike the right balance between efficiency and quality of care. It seems reasonable to predict that the medical staff will feel more confident with one of its own in charge and will be more likely to give administration the benefit of the doubt.

Most physicians are independent, small business entities accustomed to running their own practices. Many are very successful and have developed a keen business sense. Hospitals can benefit by bringing physician managers into new ventures, contracting, and related activities. For instance, a large not-for-profit medical center sought out a physician who was known for his sound business practices to be chairman of the board of the center's newly formed for-profit corporation. It wanted the benefit of his business acumen as it moved into new profit-making ventures.

Weaknesses

The physician managers' knowledge of health care generally is offset by a lack of training in management, as noted earlier. The traditional track that has led physicians into management is one of gradually increasing responsibility. Often they will find they have worked up from chairing a committee to being paid to manage and possibly spending the majority of the time managing. Because the climb into management is gradual and often unplanned, the physician managers rarely have any formal education in that field.[12] Contrary to what many physicians think, management skills are not just common sense; nor are they intuitive. They must be learned and practiced.[13]

The gradual path that brings physicians into management is fertile ground for the effects of the Peter Principle. Just as happens in all types of management organizations, hospitals may choose physician managers more for their clinical expertise than for their management potential.[14]

The AAMD developed a profile of physician managers' behaviors and leadership styles. It tested 800 physician managers, using three assessment tools. Physician managers were found to exhibit a number of behaviors that are ineffectual and counterproductive in the management role.[15]

The most significant finding was physician managers' behavior when faced with conflict. They are uncomfortable with conflict and stress and have strong tendencies to withdraw from it. However, they are not willing to admit their high level of discomfort. Therefore, in an attempt to control their uneasiness and protect themselves, they switch to an authoritarian style of behavior. This in turn leads to more conflict, and a vicious cycle begins. Display of this behavior pattern in the normal physician-patient relationship is understandable. Authoritarian behavior and masking of uncertainty are effective responses to patient care crises. On the other hand, this type of response to conflict in management relationships is destructive.[16]

A related behavior pattern when physician managers are faced with conflict is what has been characterized as the "stubborn fighter" style. The physicians make it clear that they intend to win and that the other party will lose. They do not allow room for alternative solutions that let both parties win.[17] Most nonphysician health care professionals can readily describe encounters with this type of physician behavior. One technician who is accustomed to dealing with physician managers as clinical directors said, "There's no compromising with them. If a doctor wants something and I disagree, he just stares. He expects me to give in. He doesn't even consider the possibility that he won't get what he wants." Physician managers need to learn alternative ways of dealing with the conflicts and stresses that are inevitable in management.

The physician managers were judged to have a middle-of-the-road leadership style. They typically use traditional bureaucratic methods, such as majority vote decision making. These methods lack creativity but are viewed as "safe" from their clinical perspective.[18]

The leadership area in which physician managers fall down the most is evaluation. Few managers enjoy giving people negative feedback, but physician managers find it so uncomfortable that they avoid evaluation to an extreme degree.[19] Too many postpone evaluations, hand them off to someone else to do, or fail to do them at all.

Although Beth Israel's Dr. Rabkin sees a trend toward increasing numbers of physician managers, especially CEOs, he suggests that some gaps in their training and experience will be hard to overcome. For instance, physicians do not expect to be managed and do not accept readily anyone else's right to do so. On the other hand, professional managers accept being supervised as an inherent part of working in an organization.[20] Physician CEOs may quickly find themselves out of a job if they do not recognize that the board is their management.

In contrast to physician managers' experience as small business entities, their experience in the financial and administrative activities peculiar to large institutions is minimal. Physician CEOs whose institutions are considering a new bond issue will not find much guidance from their experience as private practitioners or as academicians. The policies and procedures large organizations institute in order to achieve consistency may be viewed by physician managers as unnecessary bureaucracy. For instance, an individual practitioner may be able to get away with firing an employee without documenting good cause. A hospital, on the other hand, will require its managers to go through certain steps first to be sure that the employee is treated fairly and that the hospital will be able to defend its actions.

CHALLENGES OF THE PHYSICIAN MANAGER ROLE

Physicians' perceptions of the managerial role exacerbates their weaknesses as managers. Most do not recognize that the manager's role is significantly different and requires different skills. New physician managers often fail to realize the extent to which they are unprepared to manage and that their training and experience actually have preconditioned them against the role they are taking on. Traditionally physicians have seen management roles as unimportant, second-class, and lacking in intellectual challenge. They find support for their viewpoint in the lower pay that managers earn. Physician managers tend to identify themselves as doctors, not as managers. These perceptions interfere with their ability to perform well in the management role.[21]

Even though most physicians view management positions as uninteresting or less difficult than clinical work, they find many challenges in the physician manager role, not just those that every health care manager faces but also those specific to the manager who is a physician:

- There is the challenge of managing other physicians. Doctors resist being managed; that the manager is a fellow physician is not sufficient to overcome the resistance.[22]
- There is the challenge of balancing the cost-quality equation that often has physicians and managers at each other's throats. Physician managers have reason to support both sides but must find a way to attain their own equilibrium.[23]

- There is the related challenge of living up to the expectations from both sides that the physician managers will bring the other side around to their way of thinking. Doctors expect that the physician managers will be their representative and will deliver on all of their desires. Administrations expect that the physician manager will get the doctors to fall in line with administration's views.[24] The beleaguered physician manager may feel like a lion tamer between two rows of snarling beasts.

- There is the challenge of sorting out the internal conflict of wearing two hats.[25] Pity the physician managers who act "like a doctor" when with physicians, then must eat their own words when they look at the situation from the viewpoint of their management responsibilities.

The challenges of the physician managers' role suggest that maintaining competence and achieving a high degree of success in both roles is extremely difficult and, some would say, impossible.

Most physician managers maintain some clinical practice. The reasons for maintaining the dual role range from needing the gratification of patient care to having time available because the management role is part time. The most important reasons are to maintain credibility as clinicians and to keep open the option for a return to full-time practice. A viable and functioning practice is better protection than a golden parachute. Despite consciously choosing their dual role, those who continue to practice pay for it with tension and ambivalence about their roles.[26] What do physician managers do when their patients get sick during their management time? Whether they choose to have colleagues see the patients or to put aside their management responsibilities to see the patients themselves, they will feel guilt and failure on one side or the other.

As noted, the two major issues for physician managers who continue to practice are (1) maintaining clinical competence and (2) achieving credibility as a manager. Maintaining clinical competence requires both constant practice of existing skills and learning new information and techniques. As physician managers decrease their patient volume, they start to worry about losing their abilities. Are they doing more harm than good by trying to continue to practice? They also worry about their credibility as managers. Clinical competence will not make up for a lack of management training and ability. They must build their credentials in management and prove themselves as leaders.[27]

EDUCATION FOR MANAGEMENT

Physicians have a place in management, but a review of their weaknesses makes it clear that they are not a panacea for the ills of the health care system. Their presence can be counterproductive if they do not learn to manage well.

To be competent managers, physicians must be educated in management skills, yet most have only on-the-job-training. To truly benefit from the unique potential of physician managers, wide-ranging changes in their education must be prescribed. It is incumbent upon the physician managers to take the first steps. However, the hospital and others must assume some responsibility in ensuring that the contributions of physician managers are maximized through appropriate basic and continuing management education.

Physician Managers

It has been said that good managers are born, not made. Physicians who believe and rely on that axiom had better be so lucky or so talented that reality does not enter in. Henry Hood, M.D., president of the Geisinger Foundation and chairman of the Geisinger Medical Center, Danville, Pennsylvania, says: "Physicians have a right to be health care chief executive officers, as long as they prepare themselves."[28] Physicians interested in management can begin by recognizing their need for management skills. Then, by setting goals and developing a management education plan, they can aim to achieve competence in management as well as in medicine.

One path is to pursue graduate education in health care or business administration. However, given that most physician managers are holding down two jobs, it is unlikely that many will take the time to get an MHA or an MBA. More creative approaches are necessary. Many educational offerings for physician managers are available, ranging from intensive seminars of several weeks at major universities to "overnight wonders" with limited subject matter. The physician managers should choose courses wisely and with their education plan in mind. Most brief seminars provide a few good ideas but not a comprehensive, cohesive management education.

Role models are important, and often critical, to the developing managers. Since most of them have only other untrained physician managers as role models, the managerial weaknesses discussed previously are likely to be reinforced.[29] The physician managers should seek out accomplished managers, M.D. or not, as mentors.

The physician CEOs must realize the importance of a strong and supportive board, even though they may reject its "advice and counsel." A good board can be of invaluable assistance in the learning process.

Hospitals

Hospitals interested in developing physician managers, whether at the level of committee chair or senior executive, will have to make a conscious effort to do so. The first step is to choose a core group of physicians and convince them that they can make a difference in the course of the hospital if they are good managers. Together, the senior manager (physician or not) and the physicians should create a formal education plan, including a budget for tuition and travel. Sending some of the nonphysician managers along with the doctors to educational experiences will build a common knowledge base and increase the likelihood that what is learned will be applied.

The development of physician managers goes beyond formal education, however. They must be treated like managers and included in planning, decision making, and information sharing to the same degree as nonphysician managers at similar levels. They should be held accountable for management goals and responsibilities. This often is difficult, but exempting them undermines their development.

Hospitals willing to give management responsibility to physicians and to train them to be able to live up to those responsibilities will benefit from a higher-quality management team and greater rapport and respect from the medical staff.

Medical Staffs

Hospital medical staffs can take a giant leap forward in the effectiveness of their own functioning by expecting their officers, departmental heads, and committee chairs to manage well. Each position should have a set of performance standards, including measures of effective management. New appointees should be oriented to their responsibilities and helped to gain whatever skills they need to meet them. As stated earlier, the simple fact that individuals are good clinicians is no guarantee that they will be effective as managers.

Professional Societies

According to Richard S. Wilbur, M.D., executive vice president of the Council of Medical Specialty Societies, "Until and unless administration is recognized as a valid field of physician specialization, it is inevitable that leadership in health care will be assumed by non-physicians. The skills which have allowed a physician to run a one or two person office, are grossly inadequate for dealing with the ever more complex health care organizations."[30] The concept and desirability of a specialty board in administrative medicine has been discussed in other forums as well, but has not yet gained wide support.[31]

As an attempt to fill the gap between the demands of the physician manager role and the general lack of management skills among doctors, the AAMD together with the American Group Practice Foundation developed the Physician in Management educational program series. Since 1977 they have been producing a pair of five-day seminars given regularly at various sites around the country. The first part educates the physician managers on their role, the second presents basic skills such as decision making, goal setting, and leading meetings.[32]

Many other professional organizations have recognized the need for management education for physicians. The A.M.A. Leadership Conference is a prime example of the type of program available to physician managers through their professional societies. Such organizations need to expand their management offerings and give Continuing Medical Education (CME) credit for traditional management courses taken by physician managers.

Hospital Administration Schools

Schools of hospital administration are willing to accept physicians as students, but these institutions need to recognize that most physician managers will not yet be able to devote themselves to a traditional graduate program. Programs should be developed that meet their working schedule and concentrate their training in areas in which they are weakest.

The role of the physician manager should be part of the M.H.A. student's curriculum on hospital organization. The nonphysician managers need to know the strengths and weaknesses of the physician managers and how to make the most out of working with them.

Medical Schools

Management skills must be incorporated into the basic medical school curriculum. Even physicians who never devote a significant portion of their time to management will benefit from and, it is to be hoped, have more appreciation for management skills. They will better understand the work of hospital managers, both physician and nonphysician, and undoubtedly will find the skills useful in managing their own practices.

A LOOK AT THE FUTURE

In sum, after several decades of declining numbers of physician administrators, the trend has reversed and physicians are returning to health care management. With the revolution in delivery of care, the increasing surplus of physicians, and the stresses resulting from these factors, doctors will be sought for and will seek roles in all levels of management.

Physicians generally are assumed to be inept managers. Certainly the classic medical training does not prepare them to be professional managers and, in fact, produces fundamental weaknesses in their management skills. On the other hand, their experience in patient care and knowledge of physician-patient relationships gives them a tremendous advantage. In the changing health care environment, physicians who are effective managers will find unlimited opportunities.

The potential for increasing numbers of physicians in health care administration comes at a time when the industry is retrenching. This clearly poses a threat to the career paths of nonphysician managers. It is incumbent upon the management structure to turn this threat into an opportunity.

Physicians who manage or are interested in managing must take the lead in developing their own management skills and in convincing their profession to recognize health care management as a legitimate medical specialty. Hospitals and other organizations also have an obligation to educate the physician managers in order to maximize their potential contributions to the delivery system.

NOTES

1. Summary Report of the Graduate Medical Education National Advisory Committee: To the Secretary, Department of Health and Human Services, September 30, 1984.

2. James B. Gantenberg, "Who Leads America's Hospitals?" *Hospital and Health Services Administration* 30, no. 2 (March/April 1985): 50–52.

3. Arthur Young & Company, "Trend Toward Doctor Administrators Fueled by Hospital Cost Pressures" (New York, December 19, 1984, Mimeographed), 1.

4. Carel N. Hurless, Administrative Assistant, The American College of Physician Executives and The American Academy of Medical Directors, personal communication to Lois Tow, San Francisco, April 16, 1985.

5. Gantenberg, "Who Leads," 47–48.

6. Jerry Royer, "Why Physicians Move Into Managerial Roles," in *The Physician in Management,* ed. Roger Schenke (Falls Church, Va.: The American Academy of Medical Directors, 1980), 25–26.

7. William F. Hejna and Cheryl M. Gutmann, "Environmental Forces Expand Management Slots for Physicians," *The Hospital Medical Staff* 12, no. 4 (April 1983): 2–3.

8. Emily Friedman, "Trustees and Physician CEOs: Possibilities for Partnership," *Trustee* 39, no. 2 (February 1985): 32.

9. Arthur Young, "Trend," 4.

10. David S. Forkosh, "Good Doctors Aren't Always Good Managers," *The Hospital Medical Staff* 11, no. 5 (May 1982): 3.

11. Bruce E. Spivey, "The Physician as Administrator: An Emerging Trend." Paper presented at the 55th annual convention of the Association of Western Hospitals, Los Angeles, April 24, 1985.

12. Paul Torrens, "Physician's Perceptions of the Managerial Role," in *The Physician in Management,* ed. Roger Schenke (Falls Church, Va.: The American Academy of Medical Directors, 1980), 20–21.

13. Forkosh, "Good Doctors," 3.

14. Jerry Royer, "The Dual Role Dilemma: A Perspective from Medicine," in *The Physician in Management,* ed. Roger Schenke (Falls Church, Va.: The American Academy of Medical Directors, 1980), 81.

15. Michael E. Kurtz, "A Behavioral Profile of Physicians in Managerial Roles," in *The Physician in Management,* ed. Roger Schenke (Falls Church, Va: The American Academy of Medical Directors, 1980), 33–35.

16. Ibid., 38–39.

17. Ibid.

18. Ibid., 40.

19. Ibid.

20. Friedman, "Trustees," 32.

21. Torrens, "Physician's Perceptions," 19–23.

22. Carl Slater, "Challenges of the Physician Manager's Role," in *The Physician in Management,* ed. Roger Schenke (Falls Church, Va.: The American Academy of Medical Directors, 1980), 74.

23. Ibid.

24. Ibid.

25. Ibid., 74–75.

26. Royer, "Dual Role," 79–80.

27. Ibid., 81–82.

28. "MDs Have A Right to be Healthcare CEOs," *Modern Healthcare* 13, no. 6 (July 1983): 90.

29. Kurtz, "A Behavioral Profile," 41.

30. Richard S. Wilbur, "CMSS Annual Board of Directors Planning Meeting," *Council of Medical Speciality Societies Executive Report* 8 (May 1985): 3.

31. American Board of Medical Specialties, *ABMS Record* (February 1986): 12–13.

32. W. Grayburn Davis, Shattuck W. Hartwell, and John W. Pollard, Preface, *The Physician in Management,* ed. Roger Schenke (Falls Church, Va.: The American Academy of Medical Directors, 1980), x–xi.

The CEO's Perspective on Leadership Styles: Strategies for Success

Donald S. Buckley

14

Health care executives of the future must adapt styles and strategies of leadership that will be commensurate with the environments expectable then. Many of today's leaders unfortunately may be unemployed spectators of the health care scene in the future. The mid-1980s witnessed an extremely high turnover of hospital CEOs, along with many who were accepting early retirement. It is essential that executives be able to identify their appropriate leadership style, to know when to use each particular element and what strategies to use in implementing them in the future.

This chapter reviews past and present health care environments and examines the similarities and the contrasts in what has taken place. The sixties and seventies saw the passage of Medicare and Medicaid legislation, the development of the regional medical programs, and the establishment of additional medical schools. The seventies was an era of additional regulations in an effort to contain costs. During that time the major malpractice crisis arose to add to those costs.

A LOOK AT THE ENVIRONMENTS

The relatively placid environment of the early 1960s offers a strange contrast to the turbulence that has emerged since. Restrictions and regulations were almost nonexistent compared with the more recent era beset by political influences and heavy controls. During the earlier period, there was little competition between hospitals, and each institution observed its own service area boundaries. Marketing was unheard of.

Now, the industry is in the midst of a fiercely competitive era, with high-pressure Madison Avenue marketing techniques and strategies to invade competitors' territories. The change from cost reimbursement to prospective payment has brought about another new environment. This has confronted

CEOs with the risk of their institutions' failing because of the uncertainties of the financial systems. The consumers of health care no longer are the patients'; they are the businesses and industries that employ them and provide health benefits through health maintenance organizations (HMOs), preferred providers organizations (PPOs), and other alternative delivery arrangements.

STYLES OF LEADERSHIP

As the environment has changed, so also have the styles of leadership required of CEOs. Leaders in the sixties tended to be relaxed, often were social leaders, and assumed little professional risk; now, by necessity they have become demanding and operate in a structured, corporate setting. Health care leaders in a sense are entrepreneurs, experiencing high risks and being required to resort to aggressive tactics. These characteristics of leadership style are blurring the CEOs' role as seen by the governing board because they are so different from the earlier decades.

Leadership is a nebulous and ill-defined characteristic. Bennis and Nanus state that "probably more has been written and less known about leadership than about any other topic in the behavioral sciences."[1] They add that "leadership is like the Abominable Snowman whose footprints are everywhere but is nowhere to be seen."[2] Leadership is not something that individuals can have bestowed upon them or that they can acquire quickly. It is a process of influence between a leader and those who follow.

Leaders Versus Managers

Much has been written and debated on the differences between organizational leaders and managers. Needless to say, both are necessary for success in organizations, and each has distinct characteristics. Leaders must focus on the emotions and organizational values, on commitment to the organization, and on aspirations for its success. They must set the institution's direction and serve as its catalyst or glue. In contrast, managers must focus on physical and human resources, capital availability, raw materials, and technologies. These elements are tangible and primarily materialistic. These components are melded into the fiber of the organization and transformed into the components of leadership.

Who Is a Leader?

Leaders in part are crystal ball gazers with their attention focused on goals and ideals of the future. They benefit from experiences, including their failures as well as their successes. A retrospective analysis gives a 20/20 view of events.

Depth perception is essential because beneath each issue is a direction for the future. The meaning behind others' actions can help leaders in making the decisions of the future. Finally, leaders must be willing to retract, revise, and change. They cannot insist on maintaining pride of authorship and be unwilling to end projects, programs, and activities if their continuation is not justified.

Views of the Experts

In determining the appropriate styles of leadership and successful strategies for future environments, CEOs can benefit from authors such as Peter Drucker, Thomas J. Peters, and Robert H. Waterman, as well as Warren Bennis and Bert Nanus who authored *Leaders: The Strategies for Taking Charge.* Styles of leadership applicable to health care are also presented by Paul Hersey and Ken Blanchard in *Management of Organizational Behavior Utilizing Human Resources.*

Peters and Waterman promote principles of leadership that stimulate executives to be action oriented, to know their customers, and to provide an autonomous and entrepreneurial environment.[3] Being action oriented requires hospital governing boards to make prompt and expedient decisions, and to have such decisions facilitated by concise and meaningful information from the CEOs. Innovation and entrepreneurship are being shown by hospitals that diversify into activities which are uncommon for hospitals to enter, such as manufacturing disposable containers for hospital supplies and providing laboratory services to industries on the job site. Innovation is measured by the degree to which something is recognized and commonly accepted as being done by a hospital. All of these principles can be the bases of leadership styles for health care executives.

Bennis and Nanus address four elements of leadership:

1. The talent of vision in focusing on the institution's mission. This vision must be result oriented, must be given an understandable meaning by the leaders, and must be communicated clearly to the staff. An understanding of the vision is essential in order to obtain participation in and "ownership" of the organization's mission.
2. The talent to serve as "social architect." This individual must understand the silent variable that translates the idiosyncrasies, nuances, and confusion of an organization's life into a meaningful entity. This architectural pattern will serve as the guide to who says what to whom and about what. Such leaders understand their organizations and shape the

way in which they will function best. The architectural design of organizations will continue to change.[4]

3. The talent for trust, toward the organization and toward the staffs. Acceptance of the organization's message will require trust that can oil the institution's wheels and make it possible to function. Implied in this trust is accountability, predictability, and reliability.

4. The talent for self-deployment and self-evaluation. Self-deployment is understanding one's self and worth. This must be accomplished before CEOs can lead and understand those they lead. Self-deployment and self-evaluation center on personal characteristics: persistence and self-knowledge, willingness to take risks and to accept losses and mistakes by subordinates.[5]

Hersey and Blanchard view styles of leadership that change with the level of maturity and ability of the followers to accept responsibility. These styles include telling, selling, participating, and delegating. As the followers' willingness and abilities change, the leaders' use of each style will be altered. Each new situation will change the style needed with particular groups. These styles of leadership are appropriate for health care executives and apply in working with the medical staff, governing board, and management staff.[6]

Drucker's leadership styles involve innovative skills and entrepreneurial activities. It is essential that leaders dispose of obsolete and outlived technologies, activities, and projects. This requires a recognition of life spans and life expectancies of a management style.[7] CEOs must recognize the amount of innovation required for their organizations and be able to define its gaps and meet its needs. Not all organizations are receptive to innovative styles of management, so timing is of great importance. Abandonment of old styles may be required before the introduction of new and innovative ones is appreciated or accepted.

ENVIRONMENTAL ASSESSMENTS

In determining the styles and strategies of leadership for the future, CEOs must recognize the current environments and those that are likely to present themselves. Environmental pressures occur from both without and within organizations. The external environments consist of governments, the various publics, businesses and industries, professional organizations, and educational institutions. Internal environments consist of hospitals' governing boards, medical staffs, management staffs, and employees. Each of these components affects and helps to shape leadership styles. As the environments change, so must those styles.

Assessment of the External Pressures

Pressures from the federal government include changes in prospective payment systems, agency regulations on Professional Review Organizations (PROs), concerns over the increasing amount of uncompensated care, and the possibility of losing tax-exempt bond financing. All state governments involve pressures unique to each state and to each institution. These can include licensure laws, legislative changes, taxation concerns, and reduction in Medicaid payments.

Hospitals serve many publics: local schools, political organizations, senior citizen groups, and others unique to each community. The health care environment is constantly affected by increasing pressures from businesses and industries, which as major payers are, in effect, consumers of care and certainly feel the major impact of cost increases. Business coalitions bring collective pressures on hospitals to hold down expenses. Cost-containment pressures are evident in the audits of patient accounts, medical care reviews, and industries' competing directly with health care providers. In efforts to reduce costs, businesses and industries are adopting the new roles of health care providers. Their competition with hospitals is increasing and will reduce utilization and affect income.

Professional organizations and educational institutions are feeling pressures that they are relaying to health care executives. The professional organizations are concerned with credentialing, the reduction in earnings of their constituents, and the impact of the shrinkage in the demand for services. They also are concerned about the protection of their own professional turf and the impact of the entry of other professionals. Physicians are concerned about fewer office visits and the intrusion of nonphysician providers such as podiatrists, chiropractors, nurse practitioners, and physician assistants. Educational institutions have great concerns as to the continuation of quality affiliations, future sources of payments for graduate medical education, and the education of nurses and allied health professionals. These concerns center on how to maintain the quality of education with decreasing resources, limited affiliations, and a lessening demand for graduates.

Internal Environmental Pressures

The internal environment consists of the governing board, medical staff, management staff, and employees. Hospital governing boards are facing an identity crisis. They are in a state of transition and recognize that their institutions are taking new directions, entering arenas that are not related to health. Board members are experiencing a need to reassess the values to which they committed themselves when they assumed their roles. The "free care" that was given so readily is being limited now because of the need for economic survival.

Board members are seeing their CEOs becoming involved in new roles that are requiring different attitudes and mindsets. Because of concerns over litigation, boards are taking tight reins on the quality of care and feeling a greater accountability. They are finding new relationships with the medical staff, CEOs, and governmental entities. They are being forced into becoming risk takers because of changes in reimbursement and the competitive environment.

Hospital medical staffs are in a new and frightening environment and a role that they feel contains ambivalence and some schizophrenic tendencies. This role places them as both friend and foe of the hospital depending on the matter at hand. The physicians generally are supportive of the hospital's success but not at the expense of the physicians' practice. Medical staff members consider themselves both adversaries and partners with the hospital. Physicians are being held responsible for the economic viability of the institutions and yet at times are finding the facilities are competitors. Hospitals likewise are finding their physicians assuming the role of competitors by establishing diagnostic centers, urgent care centers, and other outpatient services. Physicians are concerned about the projected surplus in their field and the reduction in office visits. These concerns, frustrations, and fears have an impact on the physicians' relationships with CEOs and hospital boards.

Hospital management teams are feeling the pressures of the internal operating environment and are passing some of them along. They are finding new relationships resulting from corporate reorganizations. Management staffs are being held to a greater degree of accountability; as recompense, they frequently are being reimbursed on an incentive basis. Organizational belt-tightening and reduced demand for services are producing stiff competition between individuals on the management staffs when layoffs occur. And, finally, there are mergers, acquisitions, and takeovers. These increase management anxieties and, again, in-house competition.

Excess capacities and low volumes have a direct impact on hospital employees. Diversification, the development of HMOs and PPOs, and other changes in the health care industry are not understood by most employees, accelerating their feelings of insecurity and affecting their relationship with the institution.

THE FUTURE ENVIRONMENT

When executives attempt to envision the future environment of the health care scene, the crystal ball becomes fuzzy and clouded by uncertainty. The external environment of the future may see government adopting models of care and payment mechanisms originated by private industry. These can influence the amount and degree of federal regulations. An important factor, from the government's perspective, will be related to the status of the national deficit. The availability of funds and the continuation of programs cannot be known until this is under control.

As governmental concerns have an impact on hospitals, with resultant pressures on operations, the various publics will feel the repercussions. Difficulty in getting into the system and limitations on the amounts of care available will adversely affect the elderly and minority segments of the population.

The publics of the future will be more demanding of institutions and more confused by the system. This will further fuel the malpractice crisis.

The roles of business and industry will be those of "kings of the health care consumers." They will be providers either directly or by contract. Businesses and hospitals will link up in partnerships for the efficient production of care at the lowest price. This could lead to questions of business ethics versus medical ethics and even have antitrust implications. The issue will be whether quality can be maintained while care is being provided at the lowest cost possible.

Competitive Forces

Competition will be greater. Hospitals will compete with hospitals, both on a multihospital basis and singly. Hospitals also will compete with physicians, insurance companies, private industry, and medical schools. Physicians will compete with hospitals, industries, and medical schools. The significant new competitors will be the university hospitals, which will increase their aggressiveness in marketing.

Alternative Delivery Systems

Alternative delivery systems will be a major force. These will consist of HMOs, PPOs, and exclusive provider organizations. Other arrangements can be expected because of the innovativeness of joint endeavors between health care deliverers and insurance companies. These arrangements and plans will be price competitive and will offer a no-frills level of care. This is being seen as physicians are agreeing to contract with providers on a salary basis as opposed to entering private practice.

Nonconventional Providers

To add to this competitive environment, there is a proliferation of non-conventional providers such as free-standing ambulatory centers, surgicenters, diagnostic centers, and urgent care centers. In addition, nutritional food outlets, tanning salons, weight loss salons, and other "health-related" activities abound on the commercial market.

INTERNAL PRESSURES OF THE FUTURE

The hospital's future internal environment will consist of the same basic elements it has had all along: governing board, medical staff, management staff, and employees. The governing body will be multi-institutional, with paid members, and with half or more of them coming from within the institution. These boards will be future oriented and risk takers. Of necessity, they will operate in an entrepreneurial fashion identical to their business counterparts in order to have financial viability. They will offer compensation for their chief executives and management staffs on an incentive and bonus basis in order to encourage an aggressive posture for the future.

Governing boards will have to be more business oriented and less socially oriented. Boards will be looked at as leaders of a business and commercial activity rather than of a social institution. This will cause drastic changes in their value orientation. For example, issues such as funding care for indigent patients will be weighed more carefully; in the past, hospitals were assumed to do so automatically.

The Medical Staff of the Future

Medical staff members will be more independent but will be part of macroinstitutions that will include an insurance entity and a health-providing entity or "factory component" consisting of the hospital, home health, nursing homes, and other producers of care. The medical staffs will be much more cost conscious and more competition oriented, and will be closed staffs. Physicians will be more involved in the management of the institution, but many will be better equipped through acquired graduate degrees in business.

Management Staffs

Management staffs of the future will find themselves in a multi-institutional corporate setting. This setting will utilize specialists in planning, strategy analysis, strategic marketing, organizational communications, insurance, law, and investments. Many of these specialties have not been seen in hospital management structures in the past, but the demands of the future will necessitate their addition.

Future management staffs will be more nonhealth industry oriented and will have increased relationships with local businesses. There will be increased use of information systems involving health care cost experience both internally and on a shared basis with other institutions. Because of the assumption of greater risks by management staffs, and their being held to greater accountability, there will be more internal competitiveness and striving for upward mobility. This will result from an increase in horizontal and vertical mobility opportunities.

Employees of the future will find themselves in a totally new environment. They will be faced with different value systems in an industry that will be economically driven as opposed to socially driven. Employees who are providing patient care will have to adjust to the idea of a two-tier system in medicine and to rationing of care. These two tiers will include one level of service for the full pay and another lesser level of service for those whose care is being paid on a lower basis. Some patients will receive the life-prolonging and life-comforting measures of care and some will not. The criteria for this may be age, economics, or other factors. Bioethical concerns will be of major magnitude and will have a definite impact.

Future Leadership Strategies

All hospital and health care CEOs recognize the fact that change is occurring but they must face the question of how their style of leadership and strategies must change to meet the new pressures and challenges. Flexibility in leadership will be required to match their executives' approaches with the conditions dictated by the changing conditions.

Governmental Environments

Health care leaders must build coalitions with leaders in government at all levels. These coalitions must involve board members, medical staff, and management as well as members of the public. Visibility of health care executives on governmental issues will be essential but this will necessitate taking positions and assuming risks. Differing views will be found in boards, medical staffs, and the community at large. Politically, a CEO's board may disagree with the CEO taking a progrowth stand on the local political scene but such is taken in an effort to foster growth of the institution. This could cause disharmony between the board and the CEO, but if such a position is beneficial to the hospital the CEO's position must be taken.

Networks must be established by CEOs through their boards, medical staffs, and hospital auxiliary and management staffs. These networks will be issue specific and will reach locally, statewide, and nationally on many issues. They will extend from one multihospital system to another and from one set of shared ventures to other shared ventures. The leaders must be brokers of health care needs responsible for either providing or arranging for the services to be provided. They must prioritize those needs as they address them in the governmental environment and cope with a perpetual shortage of resources. Political Action Committees could be an example of this networking involving the board, medical staff, hospital auxiliary, and administration in efforts to gain more favorable political decisions.

The Publics

The health industry's multiple publics will bring new pressures on institutions and must be addressed through innovative strategies and refocused priorities. These publics will include the elderly, political groups, ethnic groups, neighborhoods, and various economically dispersed groups. Refocusing priorities may mean giving more emphasis to the planning and allocation of resources to ambulatory care and geriatric-oriented services, such as retirement centers rather than to inpatient activities. The policy of accepting all of the charity care in the community may need to change under the economic constraints. Trade-offs may be necessary.

Another strategy is to identify and build on the strengths of the institution. These strengths may be in the governing boards, marketing programs, geriatric programs, or other aspects of the organization. They may be in people, programs, finances, or facilities. One hospital redirected its efforts toward the comprehensive care of the elderly. It operated an excellent array of geriatric services capitalizing on the existing recognized expertise and resources in geriatrics medicine.

In order to address the numerous segments of the public, small impact groups must be utilized, addressing their different and ever-changing needs, desires, and locations. These impact groups may be task-related or group-related so as to have attention given to a specific need or sector of the population. Due to the multiple health needs of the various publics, each public will be viewed as an impact group. A careful balance must be maintained in dealing with minorities, the elderly, voluntary health agencies, and others in the community. In developing additional services for a new obstetrical service at one hospital, a proper balance had to be maintained with other types of services, such as the emergency and trauma care, as well as the alcohol and chemical dependency programs. In this case, an impact group needed to be formed among the various constituencies to try to maintain a balance.

Educating the public as to what the health care system offers and how to access its various segments will become more essential as alternative delivery methods become more prevalent. The participants in this educational endeavor will include all health professionals, administrators, and physicians. One major concern is that of the medically indigent and their access to the health care system. This requires continual education from private as well as public sources such as public health departments.

BUSINESSES AND INDUSTRIES

A major component of the health care industry of the future will be involvement with businesses and other industries, building mutually beneficial coalitions and assuming positions of leadership. Networking will be a necessity and will require the utilization of specific members of the boards, medical staffs, and community organizations. Strategies of "internetting" between board members and their business colleagues will need to be formalized. As an example, "internetting" will involve the communicating of associates and colleagues of board members who are in businesses with the health industry. These business leaders with whom the health maintenance organizations are contracting are often colleagues and friends of hospital board members. This provides the hospitals an opportunity to inform and influence businesses and industries. This networking will extend nationwide through the alternative delivery systems. There is a natural relationship between board members and the business leaders with whom alternative delivery systems are negotiating. CEOs need to create an interactive mechanism so board members can serve as catalysts in introducing these programs to business leaders. One example of this is hospital-sponsored businessmen's luncheons where the board members encourage other business leaders to meet and to learn about alternative delivery systems and other hospital-based programs.

Institutions will have to refocus their priorities as they relate to businesses and industries to improve relationships, including positioning themselves for greater involvement in their health care needs. These can include joint ventures or other contractual relationships. Innovation will be essential and will necessitate the assumption of risk. An example of these joint ventures would be a hospital that joins with a private durable medical equipment company in providing this service instead of providing the service singularly.

These new relationships will require some redesigning of the frameworks of the organizations to deal with the increasing external influences and pressures. Health care organizations will include business liaison staffs and sales staff. The Chesapeake General Hospital wellness program has developed sales techniques for calling on businesses in trying to promote wellness at the work site. These persons have taken sales training courses to gain effectiveness. This can cause a change in the organizational structure of a department or possibly the hospital structure. The impact of ambulatory care has caused this hospital to study reorganizational alternatives in an effort to gain reimbursement benefits for outpatient services and for more efficient delivery of these services.

STRATEGIES FOR INTERNAL ENVIRONMENTS

The governing boards of the future will require that chief executive officers assume the role of change agents. Changes in the institutions' missions and in the boards' relationships with CEOs and medical staffs will be necessary. Boards must move in a prompt and decisive manner. This will require a more autocratic style of leadership from CEOs but this will be essential to deal with encroachment efforts by competitors. This autocratic style will require CEOs to make many decisions without consensus development with the board. There are inherent dangers in this style of leadership. The board members may feel uninformed and feel they are not properly fulfilling their responsibility. This reinforces the fact that CEOs have to be action oriented without unnecessary delays in decision making. CEOs will lead their boards in refocusing on the overall health care industry as opposed to the narrower role of the independent hospital. Boards must view the big picture in an innovative manner. An example of a governing board changing its role is in the titles and organizational structure of the board and hospital. The corporate nomenclature and realignment of board committees leads to the recognition that a board is no longer only hospital concerned but is health care concerned.

The rapid and sometimes undesirable changes in the new environment can cause dissension and disruptions in the boards. CEOs must monitor the pulses of their boards and develop cohesiveness through effective group dynamics and the appropriate styles of leadership. CEOs must recognize the development of factions and splits on the boards. The board members may feel they are losing power and authority because of changes in responsibility and authorities. This occurrence has prevented many boards from reorganizing in an effort to accomplish diversification.

Boards of the future will welcome innovation but will look to the chief executive officers as the sources of new concepts. These will not come without potential risks. The risks can be managed and minimized with adequate forecasting and careful strategies of leadership.

Hospital boards accept and promote the need for continuing education for executives, physicians, and nurses, but will find it mandatory for themselves in the future. This educational process will include technological trends in the health care industry, environmental concerns, and a constant review of the changing role of the boards themselves. These successful strategies will result only from continuing educational activities, retreats, seminars, and one-on-one discussions. Before board members will be agreeable to an innovative concept there must be trust established with CEOs. This is a developmental process and not instantaneous. This process greatly reduces the risks that come with innovations.

Continuous linkages between governing boards, CEOs, the public, the health care and medical community, and governmental entities will be essential. These linkages must be developed utilizing the existing strengths on the board. The CEOs will be looked to as the initiators of change and to help the boards to adjust to the new environment. This will necessitate a full measure of trust between the boards and the CEOs. The medical staff can often be the vital linkage between CEOs and board members as it relates to change. Medical staffs have shown through documented as well as informal ways that they support innovative programs from administration. One example of this is outreach primary care centers. Five centers were established with a supporting medical staff who helped relate the need and justification to the board. This is an important linkage between CEOs and the boards.

The Medical Staff

Strategies for dealing with the medical staffs' concerns of the future must stress flexibility and diversity. The medical staffs will be faced with insecurity and uncertainty as to sources of payment and increased competition. Because of the wide diversity of interests on the medical staffs, CEOs should establish small impact groups to deal with those factors and to help their staff adapt to the new environment. The needs must be approached individually and separately, according to geography, age, specialty, and the personal interests of the physicians. Medical staffs also must be aided in adjusting to the many changes not only in reimbursement for services but also in the total organization of the delivery of care. One example of working with impact groups is to work with the younger physicians who tend to be adventuresome in establishing a joint venture diagnostic center. This project will benefit only a segment of the physicians in a particular geographical area therefore that group of physicians tends to have a greater interest. Physicians specializing in obstetrical services could develop a program to provide medical care to the indigents.

CEOs must assume positions of visibility, of trust, and of partnership with their medical staffs. These qualities will be essential if the executives are to have credibility with their staffs and are to serve as leaders and catalysts for partnerships involving medical staff, the governing board, and management. In serving as catalysts, the CEOs must build on the strengths of the medical staffs, using their existing leadership capabilities to help implement programs and generate innovative ideas. Those on the medical staffs who have an appreciation for the broad health care perspective and understand the environment will be those who can serve as the leaders of the future. For example, our medical staff has the chairman of the AMA as a member. This individual has served as an educator and colleague on matters such as accreditation, malpractice, and legislative issues. This is a strength that can be beneficial to the overall functioning of any medical staff. The staff officers and chiefs are support individuals who should appreciate the macrohealth care issues and serve as spokespersons to the staff and board.

It will be essential for executives to listen closely to, and profit from, the concerns of medical staff members as to the future environment and as to their desires and expectations. Innovation with medical staffs will not come without risk, but that can be minimized. A positive, optimistic, and helpful attitude by the CEOs will serve to bridge the gap from confusion and insecurity to optimism and cooperative positions among the members of the medical staff. CEOs establishing strategy of availability and openness enables the physicians to communicate with the CEOs and gain confidence in working with them. This reduces the risk to the CEOs.

Management Staffs and Employees

The new environment will have a major impact on institutional values. The long-time hospital values of paternalism will give way to ones directed toward financial gains. Institutions will change their orientation from education to service to meet their need for economic survival. They also will need to adjust their levels of patient care. This in turn may require changes in the attitudes of management and employees. It also may cause confrontation and possibly adverse public reactions. There will continue to be an elite group of patients who desire extras such as gourmet meals, valet services, and other amenities.

CEOs of the future must build stable teams that work in a cooperative manner. Team building will be essential at all levels, from top management to the lowliest employees. Cohesiveness in management staffs will be the foundation for effective operation of hospitals. Team building can be accomplished through task forces developed to provide input in the implementation of the strategic long-range plan for hospitals. These task forces enable department heads to provide their insights into an institution's future development in areas such as marketing, site plans, image building, and ambulatory care.

CEO STRATEGIES FOR LEADERSHIP

CEOs must develop their own armamentariums of personal strategies to use in facing the future environments. These strategies will require them to be forward-looking, be able to abandon ideas that have become outmoded, and be willing to communicate. Personal strategies that may be beneficial are:

- develop administration and medical "think tanks" to generate new and innovative ideas for the future.
- use community networks that provide a superstructure for hospitals in an effort to support hospitals' community endeavors.
- encourage focus groups within the communities' medical staff and employees to receive general and specific feedback on hospital programs and problems.
- become more externally and community oriented so as to be recognized as a health care statesman as well as a hospital administrator.
- recognize that CEOs provide leadership for medical staffs and governing boards as well as their entire organization. CEOs should try to understand the needs, desires, and abilities of these groups.

Concepts for the future must be incorporated into the institutions' goals and objectives. CEOs must remain flexible, adaptable, and totally oriented to the unforeseen changes that will accompany their future environment. The future will require risk taking, but that can be calculated in advance and thus held to a minimum. Risks can come with innovation, but success will not come without innovative action. Funds for innovative developments must be available and be dispersed wisely. Management staffs must be receptive to innovation and willing to take the accompanying risks. Negativism and refusal to be venturesome will create a pathway to failure.

Just as important as innovation is the ability to abandon projects, philosophies, organizational designs, and management styles if that is necessary. CEOs must know when, where, and how to do so. Each management decision and action has a life span and at some point must be changed or abandoned for new and creative replacements.

Bad management practices parallel that of iatrogenic occurrences in medicine when the harm comes from the treatment. Management practices and attitudes can be harmful to the organization. Such management practices arise through attitudes of defeatism, negativism, and cynicism. These attitudes are generated in management and quickly descend throughout the ranks. This can be counteracted through positive actions and attitudes established from the top and disseminated throughout the organization. These positive attitudes must be instilled into each employee at orientation by top management. The hospital's philosophy as it relates to future growth, innovation, and participation in management must be spoken from the top. This has been successful, but only through constant reinforcement by management.

Frequent and detailed communication with the management staff and the entire employee complement will be essential if effective leadership is to prevail. This communication must concern both internal institutional matters and overall health care industry issues. New priorities will be essential and their specifics must be communicated to the boards, medical staffs, and employees. One avenue of communication is a "breakfast with the administrator" held every other week. This affords CEOs an opportunity to communicate with small groups of employees from various departments within the organization. The employees have the opportunity to ask questions on matters relating to the institution.

Another important strategy will be the ability to redesign organizations to operate more efficiently. These redesigns will eliminate functions, change responsibilities, and affect all the management staff. Managers and employees must be taught to encourage this type of thought process.

In sum, the styles of leadership that chief executive officers must assume for the future will be dictated by the internal and external environments in which they operate. These styles and strategies must be future oriented and must include the ability to anticipate institutional needs, to make rapid changes, to experiment on new management technology, and to develop decision making to a high level of excellence.

In planning for the future, CEOs must constantly know the structure and functioning or the "anatomy and physiology" of their followers and the level of management maturity in their organizations. Medical staffs, boards, and management staffs have multiple subgroups with varying needs. Their styles of leadership must be fluid and must create an innovative and entrepreneurial environment.

An essential strategy will be to keep their eyes on the ball. They must not stray from the major missions of their institutions and be distracted by their competitors. CEOs will be in precarious positions on many decisions. Governing boards and medical staffs will not be marching to the same drummer because they will not always be aware of what the chief executive officers see as predictable events in the future. This will require executives to keep their boards and medical and management staffs fully aware of the goings on in the health care industry and what they hold in store for their institutions. If CEOs are too far in front of the boards with innovative and progressive ideas and the boards are totally lost or unaware of the CEOs' reasoning, there may be a parting of the ways. In essence, CEOs cannot be rounding third base, when the boards have not left home plate. Make sure the boards understand the reasoning and rationale of the CEOs' actions.

Even though they will operate in a materialistic and competitive environment, the CEOs must create among their boards and their management and medical staffs a desire for high values, proper ethics, and a concern for the patients they serve. This will require a continual analysis of decision making and of values inherent in the organization. Staffing determinations are examples of the balance of values for patient concerns and economics: fewer staff, greater profits. If fewer services can be offered and still meet the needs, the greater the impact on the bottom line of the financial report. These are decisions that reach into ethical and value systems.

The successful chief executive officers will build organizations with a vision of their mission and goals that will be given meaning and communicated throughout the institutions. These goals will require reinforcement and clarification lest they become blurred and obstructed. The executives who survive will continue to provide that clarity and reinforcement through their innovative styles of leadership.

NOTES

1. Warren Bennis and Bert Nanus, *Leaders: The Strategies for Taking Charge* (New York: Harper & Row Publishers, Inc. 1985):10.

2. Ibid., 20.

3. Thomas J. Peters and Robert H. Waterman, Jr., *In Search of Excellence* (New York: Harper & Row, Publishers, Inc., 1982:13–15.

4. Bennis and Nanus, *Leaders,* 110–111.

5. Ibid., 16–27.

6. Paul Hersey and Ken Blanchard, *Management of Organizational Behavior Utilizing Human Resources* (Englewood Cliffs, N.J.: Prentice-Hall, Inc., 1982):152–54.

7. Peter F. Drucker, *Innovation and Entrepreneurship: Practice and Principles* (New York: Harper & Row, Publishers, Inc., 1985):151.

Index

About the Editors

TERENCE F. MOORE is president and chief executive officer of Mid-Michigan Health Care Systems, Inc., Midland, Michigan, which operates Midland Hospital Center, Clare Community Hospital, Gladwin Area Hospital, and five other subsidiaries. He holds a master's degree in hospital administration from Washington University School of Medicine, St. Louis, Missouri, and B.S. and M.B.A. degrees from Central Michigan University where he has done additional graduate work in economics.

Mr. Moore is a Fellow of the American College of Hospital Executives. He is a member of the boards of the Michigan Hospital Association, treasurer of the Michigan Molecular Institute, and chairman of the board of the twenty-three member East Central Michigan Hospital Council. In 1986 he received the Regents Award for the state of Michigan from the American College of Healthcare Executives.

EARL A. SIMENDINGER, Ph.D., is president and chief executive officer of St. Luke's Hospital, San Francisco, California. He was formerly the vice president of University Hospitals of Cleveland, Ohio. He holds a doctorate in organizational behavior from Case Western Reserve University, a master's degree in hospital administration from Washington University School of Medicine, St. Louis, Missouri, a master's degree in industrial engineering from Cleveland State University, and a bachelor of science degree in business administration from Ashland College.

Dr. Simendinger is a Fellow of the American College of Hospital Executives and a member of the American Institute of Industrial Engineers. He is also a reviewer for the *Journal of the American Medical Association* and the *Journal of Clinical Engineering*.

About the Contributors

ROBERT C. BILLS is president of Valley Presbyterian Medical Center, Van Nuys, California. He received a bachelor's degree from the University of California and a master's degree in hospital administration from Northwestern University.

DONALD S. BUCKLEY is president, Chesapeake General Hospital, Chesapeake, Virginia. He received a bachelor's degree from the University of North Carolina and a master's degree in hospital administration from the University of Minnesota.

NEWELL E. FRANCE is president of Tampa General Hospital, Tampa, Florida. He received his bachelor's and master's degrees from Northwestern University.

DAVID A. GEE is president of the Jewish Hospital, St. Louis, Missouri. He received a bachelor's degree from DePauw University and a master's degree from Washington University.

PAT N. GRONER is president emeritus, Baptist Regional Health Services, Inc., Pensacola, Florida. He received a bachelor's degree from Baylor University and a doctorate from East Texas Baptist College. He also holds several honorary doctorate degrees.

KEVIN G. HALPERN is president and chief executive officer of Cooper Hospital/University Medical Center, Camden, New Jersey. He received a bachelor's degree from Long Island University and a master's degree in health care administration from New York University.

SHELDON S. KING is president, Stanford University Hospital, Stanford, California. He received a bachelor's degree from New York University and a master's degree in hospital administration from Yale University.

WILLIAM C. MASON is president and chief executive officer of Baptist Medical Center, Jacksonville, Florida. He received a bachelor's degree from the University of Southwestern Louisiana and a master's degree in hospital administration from Trinity University.

BOONE POWELL, JR., is president, Baylor University Medical Center, Dallas, Texas. He received a bachelor's degree from Baylor University and a master's degree in hospital administration from the University of California.

J. LARRY READ is the chief operating officer of St. Luke's Hospital, Jacksonville, Florida. He received a bachelor's degree from Lamar University of Beaumont, Texas, and an MHA from Washington University School of Medicine in St. Louis, Missouri.

AUSTIN ROSS is executive administrator of the Virginia Mason Medical Center, Seattle, Washington. He received both bachelor's and master's degrees in hospital administration from the University of California.

ARLENE A. SARGENT is associate professor, Holy Names College, Oakland, California. She received a BS degree from the College of St. Catherine, a master's degree from the University of Minnesota, and an Ed.D. degree from Northern Illinois University.

KEN W. SARGENT is president and chief executive officer of Alta Bates Corporation, Berkeley, California. He received a bachelor's degree from Yale University. He also received a master's degree in hospital administration from the University of Minnesota and a master's degree in business administration from Loyola University.

BRUCE E. SPIVEY, M.D., is president, Pacific Presbyterian Medical Center, San Francisco, California. He received a bachelor's degree from Coe College, a master's degree from the University of Iowa, a master's degree from the University of Illinois, and a medical degree from the Iowa College of Medicine.

CAROL D. TEIG is director of planning at the Jewish Hospital, St. Louis, Missouri. She received her bachelor's, MA, and MHA degrees from Washington University.

LOIS M. TOW is business manager, the department of opthalmology, Pacific Presbyterian Medical Center. She received a bachelor's degree from Dartmouth College and a master's degree in health services administration from Arizona State University.

ROBERT L. WALL is director of Cabarrus Memorial Hospital, Concord, North Carolina. He received a bachelor's degree from Guilford College and a master's degree from the University of North Carolina. Mr. Wall also received a certificate in hospital administration from Duke University.

DAN S. WILFORD is president of Memorial Health Care Systems, Houston, Texas. He received a bachelor's degree from the University of Mississippi and a master's degree in hospital administration from Washington University.